This Circuit Rider sketch, which appears here and at each chapter head, has been so widely used through our area in many copied forms. It is probably the second most important symbol to this writing. A production of artist Dudley Ward, it appeared first in the Methodist magazine Together. It is used here with permission of Mr.Ward.

Official Pennsylvania Historical Marker. It stands along Route 272 north, opposite and visible from the Boehm's Chapel. Its cost was a gift to the Chapel from the "Boehm's Family." It was unveiled and dedicated at a special ceremony on April 29, 1984. Its wording was submitted by members of the Boehms Chapel Society.

THE TEMPLE OF LIMESTONE
- A History Of Boehms Chapel -
1791 - 1991

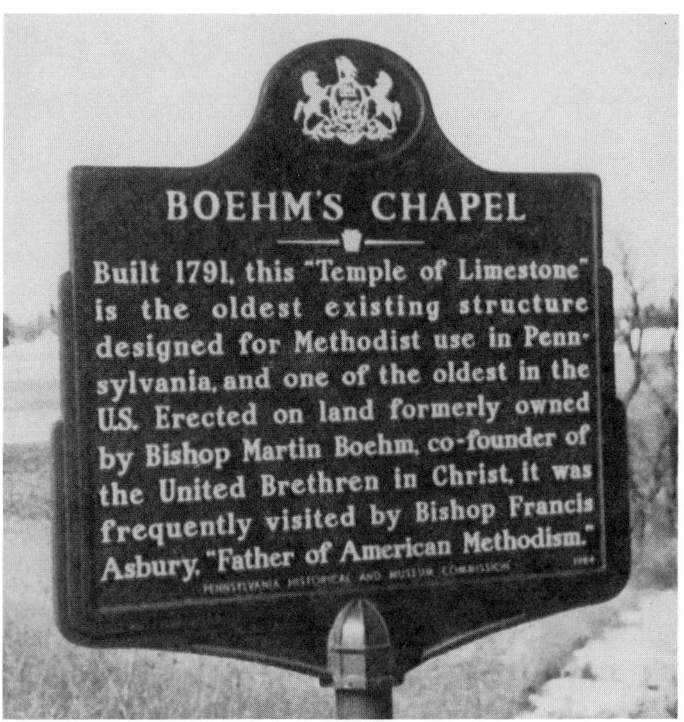

"Hail Boehms Chapel
The Temple Of Limestone
Strong and Enduring..."

Abram W. Sangrey
Lancaster, Pennsylvania

1991

TO

My Memories Of

Martin and Henry Boehm

Published June 1991.
Printed and bound in Lancaster, Pennsylvania.

Published for the Boehms Chapel Society, and the Eastern Pennsylvania Conference Historical Society, The United Methodist Church.

ISBN 0-9623805-1-2
Library of Congress Catalogue Card Number 91-61442

Typeset by Secretari-All, Lancaster, PA.
Photos prepared by Eckert Photography, Leola, PA.
Printed by Brookshire Printing, Inc., Lancaster, PA.

The Cover. This beautiful interpretation of the 1791 Boehms Chapel was painted by a local artist, Ms. Joann Hensel of Millersville. An active member of the Pennsylvania Watercolor Society and the Lancaster County Art Association, she commissioned this painting to the Boehm's Church in 1976. It is reproduced here with permission.

C O N T E N T S

LIST OF ILLUSTRATIONS

Cover

<u>Some Abbreviations In This History Writing</u>

UMC	-	United Methodist Church
Menn.	-	Mennonite Church
UBC	-	United Brethren Church
Rem.	-	*Reminiscences*, by Henry Boehm, 1875
Hist. '43	-	*History of Boehms Chapel*, 1943
BCS	-	Boehm's Chapel Society
A & H	-	Archives and History

SOME FIRST WORDS

Preface

The preface to my 1943 writing[1] is of interest in the context of this new edition. It said:

In the preparation of this history an attempt has been made to gather all the available materials which relate directly to the one hundred and seventy years history of Boehms Methodist Episcopal Church.

At some points these are summarized; at others they are given in full. Now in permanent form, these facts which have never been collected before are no longer in danger of being lost. The compiler has attempted, furthermore, to bring to light items of historic value contained in the few records and articles not easily obtainable.

Thanks are hereby tendered to my wife Dorothy, for her assistance; and to my professor Dr. David Dunn, for many suggestions; and to the holders of records at Boehms, Strasburg, and Safe Harbor Circuit Methodist churches, for making accessible whatever records, etc., there may be.

Acknowledgements to additional sources are made to "The Philadelphia Annual Conference Minutes;" "The Methodist Messenger", J. S. J. McConnell president, September and October 1891 issues; Henry Boehm's "Reminiscences"; Asbury's "Journal"; Drury's "Life Of Rev. P. W. Otterbein"; Steven's "History Of The Methodist Episcopal Church"; Alex. Harris' "Biographical History Of Lancaster County"; Erwin Klaus "Boehm's Chapel", which is an incomplete, brief study of this historic spot, written to meet term-paper requirements in a research history course at F & M; "Pioneering In Penn's Woods", The Phila. Tract Society; McConnell's First M.E. Church, Lancaster"; Lancaster Newspapers, 1891, 1929, etc.

I think the reference to the name of the church should be spelled Boehms and not Boehm's (regardless of how we pronounce it - whether in the anglicized Beam, or the more German, umlaut Boehm (see p. 37), because the church never was property of the Boehm family. This too is in keeping with the spirit of the early transaction, for the plot of ground upon which the chapel was built was given to the Methodist Church by the Boehm family.

Its Title Page said:

The History Of Boehms Methodist Church, Willow Street, Lancaster County, Pennsylvania, 1791-1943. This thesis was submitted as partial requirement for the Degree of Bachelor of Divinity, from the Theological Seminary of The Evangelical and Reformed Church in the United States, at

Lancaster, Pennsylvania, By Abram W. Sangrey, Lancaster, Pennsylvania, 1943.

Later on, June 2, 1976, at a time when again my continuing interest and concern for the research on Boehms Chapel and while reading the materials compiled in 1943, I wrote in the margin:

The saddest thing is the absence of any references to sources, references, and the subsequent absence of a more standard bibliography. Regrettably, professor Dunn did not require me to identify more accurately many of the sources, references for much of the very important, primary materials. I am also recalling, though vaguely, a large box of papers, clippings, newsletters, etc., at the Conestoga Methodist parsonage attic which I had access to then; which apparently is not available now; and, of course, I made no source-book reference to them.

Consequently, this 1991 edition of The History Of Boehms Chapel will be thereby improved. Some sources cited now were not identified in 1943. *Methodist Messenger* and other local sources are now identified as much as possible.

This new edition of the Boehms history utilizes most of the material written in 1943, all of it in new arrangements. And hopefully it is improved, with new additional material; including, of course, the current documentation of the Chapel's restoration goals, over the last fifteen years and the successful completion of the restoration this year.

This History Of Boehms Chapel seeks to bring together, with some interpretation, the background and emergence of the religious awakening which was coming to the colonial period, during the last third of the 18th century. It was greatly influenced by the historic Wesleyan Movement, and it is uniquely symbolized by the 1791 Boehms Chapel building.

It should be noted too that the subject and the title of the 1943 version as well as this writing is *Boehms Chapel* and not *Boehms United Methodist Church*. The distinction being that this is an attempt to record the significant facts on the history of the Chapel and its life; it is not the history of the present, continuing Boehms U.M. Church and its life and work. That is still another history - to be written another day - according to local-church-history-writing standards![2]

Therefore, because this is not intended to be a history of the Boehm's UMC, the cut-off date made in 1943 is the same in this version. (1943 marked the end of the writer's pastorate at Boehm's.) The obvious exception, of course, is the reporting here of the 1991 Restoration of the Chapel.

Acknowledgements

Many people have made contributions to this writing, directly and indirectly, both its idea and accomplishment. As a member of that first, fifteen-years ago Boehms Chapel Committee, receiving encouragement to write it then, especially from our District Superintendent, Bill Sharp, and my friend, Alan Holliday; but the perennial excuses and procrastination prevailed. Likewise, to my family members, especially my wife Dorothy (1943 and still) thanks for the encouragement and your patience with many inconveniences. And other, continuing, some old and some new members of the (now) Boehms Chapel Society, especially its hardworking chair, Jim McCullough. Fellowmembers of our Eastern Pennsylvania Conference Commission on A & H; and acquaintances and colleagues through the UMC Northeast Jurisdiction Commission A & H, especially Edwin Schell, Baltimore's pastor and Lovely Lane UMC Archivist; and Brian McClosky associate at the library/museum of Old St. George's UMC Philadelphia, and deceased members, Wallace G. Smeltzer and William R. Phinney. And to Bishop Susan M. Morrison of The EPC, and Conference members Frederick E. Maser and Charles Yrigoyen, Jr., for reading the manuscript and their brief reviews. The Boehm's Chapel Society and the Lancaster District UMC District Council On Ministries encouraged this publication.

Getting it into a book was assisted by the able typing skills of Violet Sollenberger at Secretari-All; and the help and suggestions in its manufacture at Brookshire Publications, reps Lew Corlew and Gary Myer. Thanks, too, to Don Eckert of Eckert Photography for suggestions and his donation of the illustrations preparations. Brookshire Publications distinctly donated the color cover for this publication.

This history was a labor of love, all told!

"The Old Blue Leaflet"

"The old blue leaflet" will always be part of the preface to a history of Boehms Chapel! It has the honor of being the first significant printed announcement about the chapel's place in our United Methodist Church history and the urgency associated with its restoration. It has passed through revision and reprinting. Its solid words and unique style are worth recasting as part of the first history book about Boehms Chapel! See Appendix G.

INTRODUCTION

The Temple of Limestone - An Overview

The following introduction to the Boehms story is based on material originally written (now edited) as a script to accompany an audiovisual presentation for use in churches and schools (see p. 113). It tells about the history and legacy of United Methodism's beginnings in colonial America, especially around the Boehms location, the historic "Conestoga" region.

It narrates the background of the Wesleyan Movement in the early settlements, and the work of the early "circuit riders" concentrating among the Pennsylvania Dutch; the ministries of Bishop Francis Asbury; and the leadership of (Mennonite-born) Martin Boehm.

The accompanying photo scenes show some of the classic Christian ministries' styles in evangelism (and "pietism") among the German-speaking settlers; and Conestoga is described as a crossroads of the (1968) United Methodist Church. The report also emphasizes the restoration of Boehms Chapel, erected 1791, believed to be the fourth oldest standing Methodist building in America.

Boehm's Chapel. It grew up with the early colonies and it grew up with the United Methodist Church.

An Old German Bible Printed in 1664
Sea Fever

It memorializes the spirit of the emerging new nation. It stands as a mighty symbol of the spiritual awakening which was coming to the churches in the second century of our nation.

For all of United Methodism, and especially the Pennsylvania and Lancaster County areas, Boehm's Chapel marks the early adaptations of the universally recognized Wesleyan Movement in England.

German Bible. While its language from the beginning was both English and German, in a real sense it taught the Wesleyan Movement how to speak German (and Dutch) in the new nation.

On land granted by William Penn to the Pequea Settlement in 1710, a group of six families established the first Mennonite Settlement and the first "white" settlement in Lancaster County.

Ship Sea Fever. At the end of the first year they chose Martin Kendig to go back home to report and to bring others. Jacob Boehm was among the second group to return about 1718.

He married Martin Kendig's sister Barbara. They obtained a 381-acre tract of the first sub-division, just across the rolling hills from the famous (Mennonite) Hans Herr House.

The first Boehm's family, Jacob and Barbara cleared a patch of land; worked the soil; shared in the honor of breaking ground for a first farm in Lancaster County.

Here they raised their children. Nov. 30, 1725, their youngest son, the best well-known Martin Boehm, was born. His family had been Mennonites in Europe for two generations.

Fascination and blessings were reasons enough for facing the ocean voyage dangers and the uncertainties of landing in the new world.

Little is recorded about Martin Boehm's early life; even less about his father Jacob, the first Boehm's immigrant. Born in the Palatinate in 1693, he came here at age 22.

But we do know that Jacob II was an apprenticed blacksmith and had the first blacksmith shop in the area.

And that Henry wrote of Barbara his grandmother, "She was very industrious and when necessary she would leave her (house) work and strike for him."

And we know they took in the traveling preachers, the "riders for the Gospel" even before there were "circuits", a most important fact for us here!

Mennonite-faith-under-persecution - not new for this generation; but for Jacob Boehm and other leaders new ideas were emerging throughout the expanding German-speaking settlements.

Wesley first said it: "The world is my parish." - The power and inspiration of "pietism" and evangelism fashioned styles of faithfulness and discipleship.

"Pioneering in pietism." - Christian discipleship to fit the followers of Christ in the new nation...proved to be Martin Boehm's calling and mission in the Church!

Its beginnings were in that same year, 1760, that organizer of a first Methodist Society, Robert Strawbridge, became a first-born of the children of Wesley in America.

The Word of the Lord was also coming to the Boehm's family, 100 miles to the west, in Lancaster County, calling for new forms in the ministry and new styles of discipleship.

Without meetinghouses and pastors, responding to that call, Martin Boehm's ministry was fashioned - following these families and their children.

Martin's leadership knew only frustration and uncertainty, until one day, while plowing and struggling in prayer, he said an experience of blessing and peace seemed to be poured into his soul.

The result of this 1759 filling of the Spirit, making him a new man, marked the beginning of Martin Boehm's legacy to history in preaching, and in his gifted leadership in the church.

His work was quickly confirmed by good pastoral relations at home, and by ability in itinerant preaching abroad. In 1761 he was advanced to Bishop by his congregation at Byerland.

Martin Boehm, influenced by the Wesleyan Movement, pioneered among the Mennonites and others, gathered with innovative practices in evangelism and Christian education.

Worship and praise in the gatherings of the faithful. History shows that these new forms provided a vehicle for the emphasis sometimes known as "pietism".

The Bible Explodes. ...Bible reading; open confession; counseling in the brotherhood; the Methodist "class-meeting"; hymn-singing; free prayer; kneeling to pray; shared testimony of personal religious experience...

...Meetings at other times than Sunday, including the evening; and in other places than the church - "Great Meetings" were a forerunner of the campmeeting.

Back home, the Boehms' houses continued as significant stopping places for the traveling preachers. Henry says that Martin's father and mother had done so in the first place!

Say rather "What Christians these women are!" Martin's wife, the first herself to experience personal witness of the Spirit, made her home a house of prayer, a place of meeting.

For at least 30 years, before 1791; the Boehms' homes, places of hospitality for those traveling in the Good News, "It captured a spirit of revival whose influence spread all over the country."

Classic persecution scene. Once more, new-nation Christians are being borne out of great protest. New faith Protestants in Europe, now followed the Mennonites into the colonies.

Martin's struggle and victory seemed to lead him into trouble. The penalty for his enthusiasm and evangelistic style was ex-communication. He was put out of his Mennonite Church.

History has made the location of one of Martin Boehm's outlying stations, at Long's Barn, Lancaster County, the most popular. In the Spring of 1767, 2,000 people gathered. Martin Boehm was preaching.

Present that day was Philip William Otterbein, minister of York Reformed Church. Otterbein came forward, folded Boehm in his arms and exclaimed "We are Brethren."

It was a dramatic meeting - each had been probing his own spiritual hunger; each giving testimony of conversion; each emphasizing styles in ministry, similar to what we've called "Pietism."

Long's Barn. Dramatic, in a friendship which united their love and life-long leadership...in the formation and final name of a new Christian Denomination, The United Brethren In Christ Church.

Back home, itinerant preachers make Boehm's a favorite stopping place. The first record of a class organized there was 1775, including the most famous of all circuit riders, Francis Asbury.

June 8, 1775, the most favored and gifted Boehm's son, Henry, was born. But, the most noted and remembered event at the end of that first century was the building of Boehm's Chapel in 1791.

A rare, original picture of Boehm's Chapel. East of the old homestead; from local fieldstone; a design suggested by Bishop Whatcoat; "In trust and for the use of the Methodists", the fourth oldest so designed.

Its story and influences are told best in Henry Boehm's *Reminiscences*. Reprinted and for sale with a companion volume *Index*. In 1875 one thousand people said it is the "richest volume in Methodist literature."

Conestoga Crossroads, Lancaster County, Pennsylvania traverses the roots of 1760-1815. Boehm's Chapel as symbol impacts nine things we can say about it at this crossroads.

Here, Robert Strawbridge 1760's organizer of one of America's first Methodist Societies - here at Boehm's he found early hospitality.

Here, Martin Boehm was born, 1725: progenitor of the first colonial family in the Pequea Settlement; father of Henry Boehm; first bishop of the United Brethren Church, and perhaps the UMC.

Here, Philip W. Otterbein, pastor of First Reformed Church, Lancaster 1752-1758; later, bishop of the United Brethren Church, said: "While at Lancaster: he experienced his own spiritual awakening.

Here, Francis Asbury was instructed in frontier circuit riding ministries among the Germans; visited regularly for 35 years; inspired and enlisted Henry Boehm, to become his traveling companion.

Here, Jacob Albright, founder of the Evangelical Society settled in 1759, in Lancaster County.

Christian Newcomer (no picture) third bishop of the UBC Church - here in Lancaster County, stood the house (the little stone one, now demolished, to the right) "where" said he "I was naturally and spiritually born."

Long's Barn stands here in Lancaster County, birthplace of "We are Brethren" fame where a "great meeting" brought together Boehm and Otterbein. Near the Pennsylvania Farm Museum at Landis Valley.

The first *German translation of the Methodist Discipline* was printed here in Lancaster County, urged by Bishop Asbury, and proofread by Henry Boehm.

Here stands *Boehm's Chapel*, 1791. A most unique description of it appears in that matchless poem which was read at Henry's birthday party. (See *Reminiscences*, p. 558.)

Boehm's home, from 1760 - "stopping place" and "home" for the greatest number of the first circuit riders - "where a spirit of revival spread from here all over the country."

<u>Boehm's Chapel</u>. The United Methodist Church, had designated it an Historic Site.

The Historic Preservation Trust of Lancaster County researcher, wrote: "It is well known that this structure is among the oldest,, extant Methodist Churches in the country. Less well-known is the fact that it is an architectural rarity, one of only two examples of a small stone church of longitudinal orientation remaining in Lancaster County which date to the 8th Century." Endorsed and recommended by our Eastern Pennsylvania Conference approved Boehm's as a National Historic Shrine, of the United Methodist Church.

Boehm's Chapel - the evolution of the 1982 Boehm's Chapel Society, its formation and support have been a source of identity and purpose for UMC, as well as the community round about.

At its Charter Day meeting, upwards of 200 people came forward to sign the charter, and a subsequent report showed $6,000 collected for the restoration project.

Restoration. We want to preserve Boehm's Chapel. And, its restoration will help to assure a responsible, effective interpretation of its use in continuing history to be gathered.

Boehm's Chapel - 1883. We want to restore it as a shrine to that movement - "where the work of the Spirit came together more often."

Let the people of God come together there again to gain inspiration and to gather power....there to reflect and there to pray. Again, the door is open because Jesus is the doorkeeper.

Here let any little ones come, for they will understand, fresh and unspoiled....

Here let the Confirmation Class come, to listen; to hear; to speak; to participate in membership, which shouts out: "Where are our hero fathers? and mothers? the prophet's do they live forever?"

Here let bride and groom come - to hear still other words from the great poem, "so did the glad outpouring of grace blend the hearts of the people, crying 'what God hath joined let no strife put asunder'."

The BCS has been at work seeking inspiration and help necessary to restore the Chapel to 1791 forms. Restoration holds for us a legacy in history filled with inspiration and blessing.

To see Boehm's Chapel restored is like listening to a modern epistle, in Asbury's words at Martin Boehm's funeral, "Let rising generations hear his voice, exhorting: to repent, to believe, to obey."

Fanny Crosby composed a hymn especially for Henry Boehm's 100th birthday party, June 8, 1875, now printed in the *Reminiscences*. Let two lines call us to prayer: "O Let the ardor of the past / Once more our souls inspire."

CHAPTER 1

A SON OF CONESTOGA

Martin Boehm was a major participant among that group of pioneers through whom the Spirit of God was fashioning a movement for change, around two hundred years ago in the Middle Colonies. We know Martin perhaps less well than Francis Asbury, Philip W. Otterbein, Christian Newcomer, or Jacob Albright. The journals of Asbury and Newcomer, both beautiful old classics, continue to assure their place in history. And Otterbein and Albright both have full-length books on their lives. True, Boehm is always mentioned (and very favorably) but always along with the others. This is the first time the details of his life and ministry have been placed in a monograph publication.

These words written in the introduction to the author's life of Martin Boehm in 1976 are still quite accurate, and the reference to the book is cause enough to suggest that you purchase *Martin Boehm* from the Boehm's Chapel Society. Copies are available. The following review of it appeared in the July 1977 *Lancaster Mennonite Historical Bulletin.*

Martin Boehm by Abram W. Sangrey, Lancaster, Pennsylvania. Lancaster District Council on Ministries of the United Methodist Church and the Boehm's Chapel Restoration Committee, 1976. 32 pages, $1.50. This booklet is a labor of love by one who once lived in the parsonage of Boehm's Methodist Church. It includes a foreword by Bishop James M. Ault and some delightful illustrations by Sue Thomas. Although pioneer preacher Boehm left no written materials of consequence, his son Henry Boehm did, and through this means something of this important churchman's life and ministry has been chronicled. From the time of his ordination by lot at the Byerland

Martin Boehm. The painting from which this printer's engraving was made is the only known likeness of Father Boehm ever produced. And the original has been lost. Son Henry Boehm, at age 86, in 1856, visited Dayton, Ohio at the United Brethren building, "looking upon the wall, I saw a portrait of my father. I had not seen it in fifty years, nor did I know it had been preserved, or that there was an image of him in existence. Here he was with his German visage, his gray locks and venerable beard. It was a very good likeness painted by a German artist for my nephew Martin Boehm, who carried it west when he went to Ohio..." (Reminiscences p. 488) The original is presumed destroyed, in a flood at the Dayton building.

Mennonite Church to the time when he formed, with William Otterbein, the United Brethren in Christ Church, Boehm aggressively preached the gospel as it flowed from his charismatic experience which came from his affiliation with the Mennonite Church and his ordination in the ministry. The proceeds from the sales of this booklet are to be used for the restoration of Boehm's Chapel. G.C.S.

The Methodist Messenger - On Martin Boehm

The Martin Boehm saga will be told in this history by two authors who want to talk about Martin. The first from his perspective as a churchman; the second as a member of his family.

Rev. Dr. J.S.J. McConnell pastor of First Methodist Church, Lancaster. 1881-1884, published the *Methodist Messenger*, a tabloid newspaper on church affairs, printed at Lancaster. Its September, 1891 issue carried a seven-column article on the life of Martin Boehm. An accompanying picture of Boehm reproduced there (and here) is the only likeness of Martin ever to appear. McConnell cites the sources used in preparation of the article.[4]

Birth and Ancestry

The Rev. Martin Boehm was born in Conestoga Township, Lancaster County, Pa., on the 30th of November, 1725. His father was Jacob Boehm, a lay elder in the Mennonite Society, who emigrated to America from the Dukedom of Pfalz, the Palatinate bordering on Belgium, in 1715. This Jacob Boehm was the third of that name in regular succession. The first was a native of Switzerland, and was a Presbyterian. His son Jacob the second, as we may call him, learned a trade and according to the custom of the country and times, traveled 3 years as a journeyman, in order that he might be qualified to enter into business for himself. In his travels he fell in with a people called *Pietists*. He was converted among them, and when he returned home he wanted to expose all formal religion and reprove sin with such boldness as to raise quite a storm of persecution. The family minister withstood him. His father reprimanded him, and the Church which exercised both civil and ecclesiastical authority, convicted him of heresy and sentenced him to prison. On the way to prison while not very closely watched by an elder brother who was

his custodian, he stepped over the line which separates Switzerland from France and became forever free from his persecutors. He journeyed along the banks of the Rhine until he entered the Dukedom of Pfalz. There he became acquainted with the *Mennonites,* united with them and became a lay elder. He had several children, the Jacob Boehm mentioned as the father of Martin Boehm, 3rd.

This Jacob the third was born in 1693, and he left his native land shortly after attaining his majority. He landed in Philadelphia and from thence went to Germantown, then a suburb, but now a part of Philadelphia, then to Lancaster, and finally settled in Pequa (sic), Conestoga County, Pennsylvania

Soon after his settlement he married a Miss Kendig, a descendent of one of the original German settlers of Lancaster County. He bought a farm, built a house, and established himself as a blacksmith as well as a farmer, the first of all the region, and worked diligently, his wife leaving her house duties at times to assist him by blowing the bellows and striking the heated iron.

To Jacob Boehm and his industrious wife were born a number of sons and daughters, Martin Boehm, the subject of this sketch, being the youngest one.

Education Marriage Appearance

The educational advantages of Martin Boehm were not extensive, but as the son of a prosperous elder in the church, he acquired the rudiments of a German and Christian education according with the views of the Mennonites whose influence he felt and whose spirit he imbibed. In addition to such a fund of knowledge as he obtained through the German language he acquired ability to converse in the English tongue, and in time secured quite a library of English books, which he read with pleasure and profit. Among these were Wesley's sermons and John Fletcher's Checks to Antinomianism. These are said to have been great favorites with him.

In 1750 Martin Boehm built a house on his father's farm, to which in 1753, he took his young bride in the person of Miss Eve Steiner, a lady born on Christmas day, 1734. Her ancestors came from Switzerland and settled not far from Jacob Boehm's farm.

Eight children were the fruit of this union, all born in the house built by their father, the youngest of them being Henry Boehm, who became a minister of the Methodist Episcopal Church, uniting with the itinerant ministers in the Philadelphia Annual Conference in 1801; the traveling companion of Bishop Francis Asbury from 1808 to 1813; the executor of the Bishop's last will and testament, and who attained the unique distinction of being the only American Methodist Minister who reached the age of nearly 101 years.

Martin Boehm is described as a short, stout man with a vigorous constitution, and intellectual countenance, and a fine flowing beard, which in his later life gave him quite a patriarchal appearance.

The picture presented here in connection with this sketch is from an oil painting in possession of The United Brethren Publishing Company, and is said to be a very correct likeness of Father Boehm.

Called To The Ministry. Conversion

In 1756 he was called to the ministry in the Mennonite Church, the call being determined by the lot, according to the custom of the Mennonite people. His call was a great surprise and embarrassment to him. He had no thought of being a preacher. He said in astonishment, "What shall I preach?" He was told to preach repentance and faith. He attempted to do so, but he stammered and stammered, and had to sit down in shame and remorse.

His embarrassment increased when after a while he discovered his real ignorance of spiritual things. A sense of his own "lost" condition came upon him and almost overwhelmed him. While plowing in the field he knelt at the end of each furrow to pray, and thus obtain relief, but the word "lost", "lost" seemed to go with him as he followed his plow or attended to other duties. At last, one day while midway in the field, he dropped behind the plow and cried, "Lord, save me, I am lost!" Then he seemed to hear the words "I am come to seek and to save that which is lost." In a moment he apprehended Christ by faith; a stream of joy poured over him. He praised the Lord, and he left the field to tell his companion of the change he had experienced.

When Sunday came and the people were assembled for worship he gave them an account of what had transpired since his call to the ministry. So he did, the same, on the following Sunday. Some in the congregation began to weep. This gave the preacher encouragement to speak of the

The original preface words about Martin's conversion said: "But you cannot speak about Martin's leadership and his gifts without first citing his own spiritual struggle, and greatest awakening, through his own personal sense of salvation. Martin was chosen by lot at age 31 to be a Mennonite Minister, but for several years in his teaching and preaching, he felt only frustration and uncertainty. Until one day, in the spring of 1759, while plowing in the field and struggling in prayer, he said an experience of blessing and peace and power seemed to be poured into his soul...'I left the field and told my companion what joy I felt'." This artist's conception of that personal experience clearly sees his plow handles as an altar of prayer. (Courtesy of Together Methodist magazine, 1966.)

fall of man, his lost condition, the necessity of repentance and faith. The effect was wonderful.

It was not long before some of the people heard with mournful looks, some sighed, others wept and said: "O, Martin, we are indeed lost!", "Yes" replied the preacher, "man is lost! Christ will never find us 'til we know that we are lost."

Became A Bishop and Adopted New Measures

In 1759, Martin Boehm was advanced by means of the lot to full authority in the ministry, being chosen in that manner a bishop also in the Mennonite Society.

In 1761 by the advice of his people, he went to the Shenandoah Valley in what was then called New Virginia, where he was brought into fellowship with the people called "New Light", who were among the converts of the celebrated Rev. George Whitfield. He became their fellow-helper and a great blessing to them, while he was greatly benefitted by what he heard and witnessed.

In fact, like Apollos, he learned "the way of God more perfectly," and when he returned to Pennsylvania, his desire to extend the knowledge of a present salvation broke through the old forms and bounds and he began to preach on weekdays as well as on Sundays. From this time he became a flame of fire, and preached with the Holy Ghost sent down from heaven. His success was wonderful and numerous were the seals of his ministry. Some of the Virginia preachers cooperated with him in holding "Great Meetings," which were designed to last several days and resulted in the awakening and conversion of many people.

Opposition and Exclusion

After a while opposition was manifest, at first, perhaps, it was without ill feeling and informal; but it was sufficient to indicate to Martin Boehm that he was too far in advance of his people to be acceptable among them.

He continued however to preach, widening the sphere of his labors and the circle of his influence until separation became inevitable. The part he took in promoting revivals, and the fellowship he held with ministers and people belonging to other churches led the Mennonites to say that they "could no longer retain Boehm and his followers that had been members of the church, as brethren, and that they should be excluded from the communion and counsels of the brotherhood."

Martin Boehm, with calmness and Christian patience when asked to desist from his course said: "He could not, but if it could be shown him he had done wrong, he would recall." When he was expelled he sang in German words of which the following translation gives the sense: "O thou triumphant King, / How dids't thou hope to bring / To man the hope of life and heaven; / Thyself to death, for even me, / Lord, thou hast given."

Met the Rev. P. W. Otterbein

Between 1766 and 1768 Martin Boehm met the celebrated Rev. Philip William Otterbein, a learned and faithful minister of the Reformed Church. Otterbein, from an intense desire to promote the spiritual life of the people, had also burst the fetters of the custom of the regularly organized churches of his day, and had gone into "the regions beyond his own parish," preaching in Maryland as well as in different parts of Pennsylvania, and rendering assistance to those who were laboring to build up the Kingdom of Christ.

Mr. Otterbein attended a "Great Meeting" at Isaac Long's six miles north east of Lancaster, Pa. The meeting was held in a large barn, which was 108 feet long and proportionately wide. Martin Boehm was preaching. Mr. Otterbein listened with intense interest.

As Boehm concluded his sermon, and before he could sit down, Otterbein, moved by an overpowering conviction of new-found fellowship in the truth, came forward, clasped Boehm in his arms and exclaimed: "We Are Brethren!" The effect was powerful. Some in the congregation, unable also to repress their emotions, praised the Lord aloud; but the greater part were bathed in tears, and "all hearts seemed melted into one."

The meeting was held on Whitsuntide, and it became a veritable Pentecost, the starting point of a religious movement destined to exert a powerful influence not only in Lancaster County but throughout a large section of the country.

The United Brethren

To this meeting and these circumstances, mentioned only in briefest outline here, do "The United Brethren in Christ" attribute their origin.

At a Conference held near Frederick City, Maryland, on the 25th of September, 1800, the United Brethren in Christ, were organized, or, more strictly speaking, united into a society which since has born that distinguished title. William Otterbein and Martin Boehm were elected superintendents or bishops.

Martin Boehm attended the conferences with great regularity from 1798 to 1809, being absent from that of 1806 and of 1808 only. In 1810 he was present in Baltimore while important measures were being considered.

Cessation of Active Labors

His more active labors (traveling, preaching, teaching, and organizing) however, ceased about 1805, when he was 80 years of age, though up to very near the close of his eventful life he occasionally preached with customary, singular magnetism and effectiveness.

During the last few years of his life (while in retirement and old age at home and near the farm there) he was an active member of the Methodist Class meeting in and around the active life of Boehm's Chapel. (Being the ecumenism that he was, it was easy for him to become a member to satisfy these requirements.) According to Henry's report of this relationship with the Methodist Class, he was also a member of the Quarterly Conference. He, of course, was an ordained minister and was used to administer the ordinances, baptism and the Lord's Supper.

Death and Funeral Service

On the 23rd of March, 1812, after an illness of only six days, Martin Boehm departed this life in great triumph and peace. Bishop Asbury's *Journal*, date of Friday, April 3rd, 1812, reads as follows:

"Friday, a cold disagreeable ride brought us across the country to Samuel Binkley's; here I received the first intelligence of the death of my dear old friend, Martin Boehm." Under date of April 5th, it reads: "I preached at Boehm's Chapel the funeral sermon of Martin Boehm, and gave the audience some interesting particulars of his life."

Henry Boehm records that the Bishop's text was Behold an Israelite indeed, in whom is no guile. Immense was the crowd; and the occasion was one of mournful interest. The

Bishop drew the character of his friend with great exactness, and that of many of his contemporaries...

(Note: Newsman McConnell includes brief excerpts of the Bishop's sermon. Omitted here, the full text of the sermon appears on page 75.)

His Last Resting Place and That Of His Wife

On the west side of Boehm's Chapel and within a few hundred yards of where he was born, rest the mortal remains of Martin Boehm and his beloved wife Eve, who survived him about ten and a half years.. Plain and now time-worn tablets mark the sacred spot.

On the smaller tablet is this record: In memory of Eve Boehm, consort of the Rev. Martin Boehm, who departed this life Nov. 26th, 1822, in the 88th year of her age.

As declared above, the second part of this report on the relationship of Father Martin Boehm to the History Of Boehms Chapel, comes from the observations and accounts of two authors, members of the Boehm's family.

HISTORY OF THE BOEHM FAMILY[5]

Boehm or Beam

When the ancestors of this family came to America, his name was Bohm or Bohme, written also as Boehm or Boehme. Both forms of the name are not uncommon in Germany and German-Switzerland today, as when the immigrants arrived in America, of these families now called Beam.

It is very difficult for an English speaking person to pronounce Boehm correctly. It is this difficulty which led the family's English-speaking neighbors and the officers of the Courts to find as a substitute the name sounding nearest like the German name as they heard it.

The English spelling of the name in the very earliest entries in the Court records is Beam or Behm. The name Boehm or Boehms is the German for "A Bohemian" or "the Bohemian" that is, a native of Bohemia. (The Beams are Slavic Czechs by race, but long residence in Germany or German-Switzerland has given rise to the belief that the family is German.)

A wonderer from Bohemia, in search of better fortunes or a fugitive from religious persecution, with an unpronounceable Czech name, came across the border and settled among his German-speaking neighbors. They then commonly and most conveniently called him "ein Boehm" or

"der Boehm(e)". The real name, if ever known, was forgotten! Even now, we call this or that person "the Dutchman" or "the Russian", etc; in the same way.

According to Herr O. Boehm, now living in Zurich, there are few Boehms now residing in Switzerland. The ancestors of these Boehms appear for the first time in the family registers of Wilchingen in the year 1620, which leads us to believe that they were fugitives from Bohemia during the Thirty Years War, in Switzerland, etc.

Three Jacobs

In their new home in Switzerland, our ancestors for a while lived and throve but not for long were they left in peace. A certain Jacob Boehm was living at peace with the community somewhere near the German border, probably in this same Canton of Schaffhausen. "He was" (to quote a family historian, Henry Boehm, his great great grandson) "a well connected and strict member of the Reformed Lutheran Church, the State Church...Jacob had a younger son who was named after his father..."

(Note: This family history also repeats here the oft-told "wandering-young-Jacob-story". It is omitted here. See part one, above for this story.)

He had several children, the third of whom also named Jacob, was born in 1693 and in 1721 was influenced to come to America by the glowing descriptions of the country given by Martin Kendig who, in September of the year 1710, had arrived at Philadelphia in a sailing vessel called the "Maria Hope", John Annis, master, which had sailed from London on the 29th of June with 94 passengers; and after a stormy voyage of nine weeks and four days, first saw the land of America. Two days before they sailed from London the following letter was written to their Brethren In The Faith in Amsterdam and is headed "Worthy And Beloved Friends".

This letter is # 2253 Amsterdam Archives, and is signed by six persons, Martin Kendig appearing second on the list. It was issued in thankfulness for the financial aid extended by the "Dear friends out of their great kindness of heart toward our journey", and is an acknowledgement of an appeal which they made to their Dutch sympathizers for contributions, "because the journey cost more than we had imagined".

All of these six signers of the letter, Martin Oberholtzer, Martin Kendig, Christian Herr, Jacob Muller,

Martin Meile, and Hans Herr, appear to have set out for Lancaster County Pennsylvania where they arrived in October, except Martin Oberholtzer, who seems to have remained in Philadelphia; and the five men were there joined by four others and these nine men selected a spot stretching from West Willow Street (sic) to Jackson Street, near the Centre Square, in Strasburg borough, Conestoga County, and was, roughly speaking, five miles long by three miles wide. Ten square miles or 6,400 acres, and for which they paid 500 lbs. sterling $2433. These were the first settlers in the County of Lancaster which is today the wealthiest farming county in the United States.

It is not a question of mere coincidence that the County of Waterloo, Ontario should be the banner farming county in Canada. The descendants of these Mennonite farmers, who chose the beautiful rolling land of Lancaster, were largely responsible for the selection, settlement, and development land of Waterloo. It is a certainty that these men (and women) knew not only how to choose the best land but also they knew how to farm it.

Driving through Lancaster Co., Pa. one cannot help noticing the frequent recurrence of the same names of villages, the same names for the creeks and rivers, the same names on the signs on the stores in the villages and towns, and the similar type of farm houses with the old-fashioned stoop and the barns with the projecting roof protecting the cattle, as one sees in the County of Waterloo, Ontario. Farm land in Lancaster County is seldom on the market for purchase; it is handed down from father to son. On a recent visit to Lancaster one was informed that only sales of land in the last few years brought $300 per acre.

Martin Kendig seems to have been possessed of more financial worth than his associates as he took title to nearly 2000 acres.

History is silent about their struggles and trials in these early days, but the Colonists were evidently well pleased with their home and this, despite the fact that they were in the very heart of Indian territory and that with the exception of a few scattered Scotch-Irish hunters and fishermen, they were the only white men for many miles around, but they had happily escaped the religious persecution to which they had been subjected in their old home. They immediately decided to send for their relatives and friends in the Old Country.

A voyage across the ocean in those days was no small undertaking and consequently they agreed to cast lots to decide who should carry the word to Europe. It fell on Hans Herr, but either because he was their preacher whose services could not be dispensed with or for some other reason, Martin Kendig offered to take his place.

He succeeded in his mission and sometime during the years 1712-1718 brought back with him a considerable number of immigrants, most of them with their families, among whom was his brother Jacob Kendig and probably several sisters. Martin Kendig became William Penn's agent for many years and was responsible more than any other one man for the introduction of German-speaking immigrants into Pennsylvania.

We mentioned before that Jacob Boehm had been induced to come to America by Martin Kendig. He also was one of this party. On his arrival in Philadelphia he first went to Germantown, then to Lancaster and finally settled in Pequea, Conestoga Township, six miles from the present city of Lancaster. Soon afterwards he married Barbara Kendig, probably one of the young ladies who had accompanied him on the journey from Europe.

He died in 1780, aged eighty-seven. His will is deposited in the courthouse at Lancaster and disposed of his considerable estate among his numerous family, of whom six daughters and four sons were then living. Following the German custom, his farm was left to his youngest son, Martin....

<u>The House Martin Built</u>

The home which Martin Boehm built in 1750 must have been of considerable size as on frequent occasions, according to his son's statements in his *Reminiscences* he had entertained gatherings of more than one hundred at a time.

When the writer of this sketch visited the old homestead in 1917, he was told by the present owner of the farm that Martin Boehm's house had been demolished some forty years before, and that much of the stone is now in a wall that is built about the garden.

All that remains of the old house is a peculiar large stone-arched chamber and the remains of the stone fireplace, which are (now) underneath the present large barn. The prospect from the house must have been a very beautiful one, looking down the valley of the Pequea

River. The farm is now given up largely to the cultivation of tobacco and fruit.

On the writer's second visit to the old homestead in 1918, he discovered in a dense thicket of locust tress and brambles a half mile distant from the house the old family burying ground and the graves of twenty-five of his ancestors. The graves were marked with headstones of field stone, with the names cut in with a cold chisel. It is of interest to note the various spellings of the name there, which includes "Beam", "Behm", Bohm, and "Boehm". The earliest stone bore the date 1725.

In May 1929 the writer accepted an invitation to unveil a monument erected by the Methodist Episcopal Church and the Church of the United Brethren in Christ in honor of Bishop Martin Boehm, his great, great grandfather. The ceremony took place beside the old stone Church erected in 1791 and known as Boehm's Church, because it was built upon Boehm's land in the Boehm neighborhood, and because the different members of the family did much towards its creation and were regular attendants there. Beside the Church lie buried Martin Boehm and his wife Eve. The building is now under the care of the Pennsylvania Historical Society (sic).

Large numbers attended from Lancaster and the surrounding counties and many were present from Philadelphia. In his remarks on this occasion, Bishop H. H. Fout of the United Brethren Church, said "The plan for a Union service on this occasion was happily conceived. The Methodist Episcopal Church and the Church of the United Brethren in Christ are united in a very similar origin. Otterbein, Asbury, and Boehm, Prophets of God, and pioneers in American Christianity, lived and wrought in the most intimate fellowship."

In the will of Martin Boehm, deposited in the Registry Office in the city of Lancaster, one clause bequeaths such of his books, as she may take, to his wife Eve, and all the remainder of his books to be equally divided between his four children, John Beam (my great grandfather), Jacob Beam, Henry Beam, and Barbara, the wife of Abraham Keagy.

We do not know what eventually became of Martin Boehm's books, but I have a letter written on the 1st of May, 1826, by the daughter of Martin Boehm's son John to her brother Adam Beam (my grandfather) in Canada, suggesting that the books left by Martin Boehm "ought now to be divided and, as you are the oldest son of John Behm, you ought to write or let me know how the division should be.

CHAPTER 2

THE CHURCH'S OLDEST METHODIST MINISTER

Henry Boehm - A Brief Sketch

For those readers who have not yet become acquainted with Henry Boehm the following brief sketch of his life is made here.

Henry Boehm was born June 8, 1775, the youngest of eight, at the old Boehm's farm in the Pequea Settlement, Lancaster Co., Pa. In his genuinely Christian Mennonite family setting, his mother a leader in spiritual achievements, and his father ordained in the Church, he mastered German and English expressions early on for both everyday language and the language of the faith of his fathers.

As a middle teenager he experienced a "backsliding" from an earlier "personal religious experience", when he left home to work away; but this he recovered fully at a religious revival meeting held at Boehms Chapel, at age 23.

Promptly he became a Methodist Class Leader, and in 1800 entered the itinerant ministry of the Methodist Episcopal Church, and with the customary, progressive steps in his ordination. His early leadership as a "circuit rider" preacher, teaching, and facilitating the scattered house meetings and church gatherings was variously appointed in the Eastern Shore of Maryland, Delaware, New Jersey, and Eastern Pennsylvania.

Henry Boehm, at the very outset, became a beloved pastor and was an effective spiritual director in his circuits. His leadership training and skills development

Henry Boehm. The history of this portrait photograph is not known. It is thought to date around 1870, when he was 95. (The photograph has a date , March 1870 written on its back side.) This framed picture is among the Boehm's collection.

for fulltime ministry came through an apprenticed relationship within the church's principal lay and clergy members (which experiences his reminiscences abound in reporting!). These include sustained relationships with his father, Bishop Martin Boehm, and above all perhaps Bishop Francis Asbury, the Methodist Church's leading spokesperson in the colonial period, over a span of the first thirty-five years.

Henry Boehm's most distinctive years of ministry in the Church are the five-year period, 1808-1813, when he was traveling companion and aid to Bishop Asbury "longer than any other". The developing years in Henry Boehm's ministry in the Church parallels the end-years of Bishop Francis Asbury's ministry. During that period, they witnessed, by the grace of God, the development and growth of the Methodist Episcopal Church in America, when its membership grew from 1000 to 214,000, a growth rate that exceeded the nation's population growth.

Between 1783 and the year of his death in 1816, Asbury visited in the Lancaster area 21 times. His first stopping place always was at Martin Boehm's farm in Willow Street.

Henry was Presiding Elder (District Superintendent) from 1814 to 1821, in the Districts of Schuylkill, Chesapeake, Delaware, and Milton. For fourteen years he was on circuits, after he left the Districts, in Eastern Pennsylvania and in New Jersey, and before his supernumerary relations (retirement).

In 1823 he was pastor of Lancaster Circuit, through and including Lancaster County and his home-scenes at Boehm's Chapel. Henry was his mother's pastor. (She died in November of that year and was buried beside Martin at Boehms Chapel.)

(Note: For a fascinating account and an introduction into the life and work of one circuit rider in those days in Lancaster County, see the description written by Henry's co-pastor, Joseph Holdich, printed here in Appendix B).

Married in 1818, he and Sarah Hill Boehm had four children. (Sarah died in 1853 and their graves are at the Woodrow United Methodist Church cemetery, on Staten Island, N.Y.

Henry spent the latter part of his life in the environs of New York City, especially close to his daughter Elizabeth who cared for him at that old age. She also accompanied him on frequent trips to the places sometimes of his earlier locations including Baltimore, Cincinnati, and in Lancaster County in the years 1856, 1867, and at age ninety-seven in 1871. On this last Lancaster visit he assisted in laying a cornerstone at a Methodist Church on East King Street.

When finally he came to the one hundredth year of his life, the nearby Conferences of Newark and New York, with his family and friends, honored Henry's long life and work in the Church with four celebrations, each attended by the Church's leading spokespersons and each with significant participation by Henry, gathering thousands of attenders.

He died December 28, 1875. The *New York Times'* tribute to the centenarian said: "...Father Boehm was the oldest clergyman in the world...that his Bible was at his coffin...and that it was his habit to read the Bible through at least once a year. He finished this year's reading about two weeks ago and his mark is now at the first page of the volume, showing that he was just about to begin anew..."

The Centenarian's Birthday Celebration

It is not possible to overemphasize or to exaggerate the enthusiasm and pride which a large group of our church lay members, clergy persons, pastors, administrators, and bishops felt and expressed to Henry Boehm, at the end-time of his life. Space limitations are imposed here, as the details must be read and studied to be fully appreciated.

It is an unprecedented report. There is a good chance that our United Methodist Church has never programmed a more appropriate or significant celebration in honor of a church leader at the end of his/her life, than that showered upon Lancaster County's favored, native son Henry Boehm, by the Newark and New York Annual Conferences, there in 1875. During that year there were four planned events in celebration of Henry Boehm's one hundredth year.

As one reads the reports of the observance, historians might ask: Why two pre-birthday anniversary events? One possible explanation is the general concern that the venerable centenarian might not reach his one hundredth birthday! It is also of interest to observe that his biographer, J. B. Wakeley, who was obviously the most active in the development of these plans, died between the April and the June meetings of that year, and therefore sadly did not see Henry's birthday!

With a view to encouraging the greatest possible reading and study of this birthday-party section of the

Reminiscences this fascination of Henry Boehm's centenary year - the following brief resume gives a bird's-eye view of the book's last chapters, arranged according to the sequences of events.

▪ *Page 494-499* sketch an abbreviation of the first, 1865 edition of the *Reminiscences*, and how it came to be written. Wakeley describes the oral-history relationship which he had with the venerable churchman, the period during that ten intervening years.

▪ *Pages 500-506* report Henry's 99th birthday celebration, June 8, 1874, at Jersey City, NJ. Its description was carried in the press of the national denomination's, *Christian Advocate*, but also copied into other religious journals in America and Europe, "showing the intense interest that clusters around this hero of a hundred years and the hero of a hundred battles..."

Henry received that day a surprise gift of an original painted portrait of Bishop Asbury; but the occasion was largely devoted to an eighteen-hundred-word personal summary of Henry's life, delivered by Dr. Wakeley, summarized in these characteristic words: "...we congratulate you on having been so long in the ministry -- seventy-three years; you are today the oldest Methodist Minister in America if not in the world."

▪ *Pages 507-520* include the details of a special, public service event, held in connection with the 1875 session of the Newark Annual Conference, the Methodist Episcopal Church, to commemorate Boehm's one hundredth year and for him to preach his (first) centennial sermon, April 2nd 1875. It records addresses commemorating Henry Boehm by Bishop E. S. Janes and by Dr. Wakeley, and others. One highlight of the event was a public display and reading of Henry's collection of his church credentials (documents) written at the times of his licensing and ordination.

▪ *Pages 521-577 on* June 8, 1875, Henry Boehm's birthday, a celebration arranged by a committee of the Newark Conference, at Jersey City, N.J. printed the full text of the event. It included a most significant 2500-word autobiographical sketch of Henry's life, read not by him but by the Conference Secretary. The address includes many human-interest reports connected with his long years of work.

Also, two hymns written by composer Fanny Crosby for the occasion; testimonial remarks and addresses from bishops, professors, and pastors; a most remarkable hexameter ode, historic poem, sketching his life and times in that genre; letters of commendation, and copies of old journals' communications received and written by Boehm; concluding with a reception held at his daughter's residence in Jersey City.

(Readers will notice the reference to it, and a singular line on the title page of this 1775 edition of *Reminiscences* "Phonographically Reported". It clearly applied to these additional 100 pages of that edition. But who can tell what it means?, and what was the early electronic device? It should arouse the interest of any communications experts among us! What recording instrument did they use?)

▪ *Pages 578-587* record the occasion of a *(second)* centennial sermon to which Henry was invited and requested to preach, this time three weeks after his famous birthday, and this time at New York City's historic John Street Methodist Church, Sunday, June 27, 1875. The church was crowded with many visitors and leaders of the denomination, including Bishop Janes who also spoke briefly.

The chapter's writer asserted "...Here was the oldest Methodist minister of the world preaching in the oldest Methodist Church -- an event which may well be called unique, an incident seldom seen even once in a century..."[6] Henry's opening words, recalling that he had first been there while traveling with Bishop Asbury sixty-five years earlier, said "What thoughts crowd my mind as I enter this cradle of Methodism! What rich and hallowed associations cluster around this original home of Methodism on this continent.

A Henry Boehm Chronology

One of my most difficult decisions, in the composition of this history, has been centered around how, best, to report Henry Boehm. He is the best-known, the most auspicious, and the leading personality of the Boehm's family. His journal, *Boehm's Reminiscences Historical and Biographical*, described at the time it was published, as "one of the richest volumes in Methodist literature"[7] tells all about Henry Boehm. Carved out of 2000 pages of personal journal materials, it is his biography. But, still, how best to report Henry Boehm here, to the readers of this history of Boehms Chapel? Not an easy question. The (brief) sketch of his life written here is for those who need a brief introduction of Henry Boehm. I urge you to read the *Reminiscences*! You too will find how "rich" it really is! (Note: Reminiscences was reprinted as one of its most commendable and best accomplishments, by the committee to preserve and restore historic Boehms Chapel, in 1982. Some words written for that reprint seem worth remembering at this point.

"This reprint of Henry Boehm's *Reminiscences* will make an incalculable contribution to our church. It brings to all of us a very rare and almost extinct book. This is the 1875 edition - the original 483 pages published first in 1865, plus the one hundred page addition - intriguing and unmatched in form, style, and content. It restores Henry's unique place among our church fathers as, "the link which connects our past with the present."[8] "...it advances the sometimes neglected fact that Lancaster County, Pennsylvania encompasses the most significant roots-and-origins area of our United Methodist Church...during that formative 50-year period, 1767-1815..."

So, the genre chosen here for this additional report is an extensive chronology of Henry Boehm, presented here as an attempt to develop a "first" in this form for Henry; and, secondly, as a tribute to one of Methodism's most beloved early reporters, who is telling us about how the Good News Of The Gospel came to the earliest Church In The New Nation.

June 8, 1775 - December 29, 1875

June 8, 1775	Birth of Henry Boehm, at the ancient residence, at Conestoga.
Aug. 6, 1781	Heard (venerated) Robert Strawbridge preach at Boehm's.
July 31, 1783	Heard (famous) Richard Webster preach "at my father's".
May 25, 1790	Heard (then Elder) Richard Whatcoat preach at Boehm's.
May 28, 1790	Took first job away from home, learned milling.
Sept. 28, 1791	Asbury's first sermon at Boehm's Chapel.
Feb. 2, 1793	Converted, "but then lost my spiritual enjoyment."
July 8, 1798	"Spiritually restored", at Boehm's Chapel. "Now I united with the Church."
April 2, 1800	"Was appointed Class Leader, Methodist

	Episcopal Church". "The Class Meeting 'strengthened, 'stablished, and 'settled me".
May 6, 1800	Visited General Conference, at Baltimore. "I became acquainted with many choice spirits".
May 27, 1800	Visited Philadelphia Conference, at Smyrna, Del. Received on Trial. "I walked sixty miles (back) home...having seen more, heard more, enjoyed more, since I left home, than in all lifetime before".
Jan. 5, 1801	Licensed to Preach, and appointed to "Itinerant Ministry" Dorchester Circuit.
May 1, 1802	Attended Philadelphia Conference, at Philadelphia. Appointed to Kent Circuit, Md. (In August, appointed to Northampton Circuit, Pa.)
May 2, 1803	Attended Philadelphia Conference, Smyrna, Del.. Ordained Deacon. Appointed to Bristol Circuit, Pa.
July 18, 1803	Invited to make a (short) tour with Bishop Asbury. Transferred to Dauphin Circuit, Pa. Preached both English and German.
Oct. 22, 1803	Visited The United Brethren Conference. Held at Martin Boehm's.
May 22, 1804	Philadelphia Annual Conference met at Soudersburg (Lancaster Co., Pa.).
April 1, 1805	Visited Baltimore Conference, Winchester, Va.
May 1, 1805	Philadelphia Conference, Chestertown, Md. Ordained Elder. His father, Martin Boehm was present.
July 5, 1806	As caregiver he witnessed Bishop Whatcoat's death at Dover, Del.
Aug. 21, 1806	Philadelphia Conference, Philadelphia.
Sept. 1, 1807	Facilitator of German translation The Methodist Discipline, at Lancaster.
Mar. 20, 1808	Philadelphia Conference, Philadelphia.
May 1, 1808	General Conference, at Baltimore. "Bishop Asbury requested I travel with him."
June 7, 1808	Start first tour with Asbury. Leaving parents at Boehm's.

Sept. 4, 1808	Preached first German Methodist sermon in Cincinnati.
Oct. 1, 1808	Western Conference, at Liberty Hill, Tenn. Campmeeting connected with Conference.
Dec. 26, 1808	South Carolina Conference, at Green County, Ga. "The old and the new (McKendree) bishops were an object of interest, and their appearance hailed with joy..."
Feb. 1, 1809	Virginia Conference, at Liberty Chapel, Va. "I had never thought of attending a campmeeting between Christmas and New Year's..."
Mar. 2, 1809	Baltimore Conference, at Baltimore. (Asbury wrote:) "I have suffered incredibly by the cold in the last one hundred and thirty miles; souls and their Saviour can reward me, and nothing else! Lord, remember Francis Asbury in all his labors and afflictions".
April 3, 1809	Philadelphia Conference, at old St. George's Church. "...14 were received on trial...14 were ordained deacons...8 ordained elders..."
May 10, 1809	New York Conference, at NYC, in John-street Church. "...by special request, I preached in German at the English Lutheran Church..."
June 16, 1809	New England Conference, at Monmouth, Me. Bad weather, "we're eighty miles behind our Sunday schedules..."
July 28, 1809	(First visit "home" enroute, after ten months away, at Boehm's).
Sept. 30, 1809	Western Conference, at Cincinnati. "We had had preaching (somewhere) nearly every night."
Dec. 28, 1809	South Carolina Conference, at Charleston. "...took a cold that had like to cost my life..."
Feb. 8, 1910	Virginia Conference, Petersburg. "...mud, mud, mud, deeper and still deeper."
Mar. 17, 1810	Baltimore Conference, Baltimore. "...(visited with) my father, preaching

"Saturday, Feb 24 1810 we reached Baltimore and put up with sister Dickens. Then I went to see my father, and he went with me to the Baltimore Conference He loved to attend the Conference, and wished another visit with his life-time friends, Bishop Asbury and Otterbein. On Lord's Day I heard my aged father preach in Otterbein's Church Of course it was in German...it was a lovely sight to behold the venerable Otterbein, my aged father, and Newcomer, all together worshiping in such delightful harmony. On Wednesday evening I preached at Otterbein's Church in my mother tongue and father concluded with an impressive exhortation and prayer. This was father's last visit there. . .

First Six Conferences

"Thursday April 18, the Philadelphia Conference commenced its session in Easton, Maryland...There was a camp-meeting connected with the Conference. There was much feeling under a sermon preached by Bishop Asbury...a number were converted on the camp-ground...This was one of the most harmonious conferences I have ever attended. Bishop Asbury wrote... 'What a grand and glorious time we have had! how kind and affectionate the people!' On Friday the Conference adjourned. My appointment was read off thus: 'Henry Boehm travels with Bishop Asbury.'" (from the <u>Reminiscences</u>, p. 282) in Otterbein's Church".

April 18, 1810	Philadelphia Conference, Easton, Md. "My appointment: Henry Boehm travels with Bishop Asbury".
May 20, 1810	Genesee Conference, Lyons, Ontario. Newly formed, its first session. "Bishops have authority to appoint other conferences...if new circuits be formed".
June 6, 1810	New England Conference, Winchester, N.H. "...the preachers all went cheerfully to their work".
Aug. 3, 1810	Start third tour to West. At Boehm's. "Asbury and father gave to each other the kiss of affection...he found 15 letters waiting this time..."
Nov. 1, 1810	Western Conference, Shelby County, Ky. "Bishop baptized a Quaker family...they make most excellent Methodists..."
Dec. 22, 1810	South Carolina Conference. Columbia, S.C. "...preached at 5 a.m. to over three hundred hearers".
Feb. 7, 1811	Virginia Conference, Raleigh, N.C. "...the Lord's prophets were greatly blessed".
Mar. 11, 1811	Baltimore Conference, Baltimore. "We went to see Mr. Otterbein..."
April 5, 1811	"I hastened to my fathers'...not seen since the summer before...Bishop McKendree preached at Boehm's Chapel".
April 20, 1811	Philadelphia Conference, St. George's Church. The bishop prayed with Dr. Benjamin Rush.
May 20, 1811	New York Conference, New York, N.Y. First elected delegates to General Conference.
June 20, 1811	New England Conference, Barnard, Vt. "my prayer...that I might successfully call souls to God".
July 1, 1811	Cornwall, Canada. Bishops long desire to go to Canada. "...he preached six times, besides numerous lectures."
Aug. 9-19, 1811	Asbury's longest stay at Boehm's. His sermon at Boehm's Chapel was Martin's

	last to hear Asbury preaching.
Aug. 20, 1811	Martin's farewell: "We shall not see each other again..."
Oct. 1, 1811	Western Conference, Cincinnati. "...3,380 member increase during the year".
Feb. 12, 1812	Virginia Conference, Richmond. "Enroute to Baltimore we toured the old historic port of old Virginia".
Mar. 20, 1812	Baltimore Conference, Leesburg, Va. "...Asbury said, as soon as Conference adjourns, have the horses ready, we must go to your father's...he had an impression that my father was dead..."
April 4, 1812	"...we passed by the new-made grave. to the old homestead..."
April 5, 1812	"Bishop Asbury preached a funeral, to a large crowd..."
April 18, 1812	Philadelphia Conference, Philadelphia. "...adjourned the 26th, after a very peaceful and profitable session".
May 1, 1812	General Conference, at New York City. "The first day was observed as a day of fasting and prayer".
June 4, 1812	New York Conference, Albany. "It was my last visit to the noble N.Y. Conference".
June 20, 1812	New England Conference, Lynn, Mass. "The session was exceedingly harmonious".
July 28, 1812	Genesee Conference, Niagara, Upper Canada. "...the War prevented us from hearing anything from the Canadian preachers".
Aug. 11, 1812	"We arrived at my mother's...Asbury wept for his old friend".
Oct. 1, 1812	Western Conference, Chillicothe, Oh. "the bishop labored with apostolic zeal".
Nov. 9, 1812	Tennessee Conference, Fountain Head, Tenn. The first session...a new conference. "Asbury was anxious to form new conferences..."
Dec. 17, 1812	South Carolina Conference, Charleston. "The Conference was pleasant...the southern preachers I ardently loved".

Feb. 8, 1813	Virginia conference, Newbern, N.C. "We had great order; great union; and dispatch in business".
Mar. 24, 1813	Baltimore Conference, Baltimore. "I preached in German, at Otterbein's Church".
April 24, 1813	Philadelphia Conference, Philadelphia. "...all preachers were examined...the Bishop answered, "nothing against Brother Boehm"...he then rose and said in his nervous and emphatic manner, "...for five years he has been my constant companion. He served me as a son; he served me as a servant; he served me as a slave".
April 3, 1813	Asbury: "...at mother Boehm's. Preached at Boehm's Chapel".
July 31, 1813	(to Aug. 10th) During this a longer visit, Asbury wrote his famous "Valedictory Statement" while at Boehm's.
April 6, 1814	Philadelphia Conference, Philadelphia. Appointment the Schuylkill District, end of first year.
May 3, 1814	Henry spent sixteen days and nights assisting with Asbury's illness care, at Lumberton, N.J.
April 20, 1915	Philadelphia Conference, Philadelphia. Appointed to Chesapeake District.
July 4, 1815	While Henry was visiting his mother, unexpectedly Asbury arrived! Asbury: "How the new, first, bridge stretches its pride the length across the wide Susquehanna!..."
April 18, 1816	Philadelphia Conference, Philadelphia. Bishop R. R. Roberts presiding.
May 1, 1816	General Conference, at Baltimore. ...voted to remove Asbury's remains from original grave to Baltimore. ...Henry joins Conference attenders for funeral ceremonies, with a "vast throng of citizens" and he was appointed "to preach the following Sunday a funeral sermon, at Otterbein's Church". (Note: See a twenty-two page memoir of Asbury, written by Henry in the *Reminiscences*.[9]

April 15, 1817	Philadelphia Conference. Appointed Henry Presiding Elder of Chesapeake District.
Jan. 15, 1818	Henry married Sarah Hill. They had four children.
April 22, 1818	Philadelphia Conference. Reappointed Chesapeake District.
April 19, 1819	Philadelphia Conference. Appointed Delaware District. Residence at Milford.
April 12, 1820	Philadelphia Conference, Smyrna, Del. Reappointed Delaware District.
April 15, 1821	Philadelphia Conference, Smyrna, Del. Again serving Delaware District.
April, 1822-24	Henry was appointed to the pastorate on Lancaster District, with Joseph Holdrich. A significant report of this appointment appears in a series of articles written by Holdrich, published in the N.Y. *Christian Advocate*, June-July, 1878. See Appendix B.
1824-1836	In this twelve-year period he served these appointments: 1824-25, Old Chester Circuit; 1826-27, Strasburg; 1828-29, Burlington Circuit; 1830-31, Pemberton; 1832, Bargaintown; 1833, Tuckerton; 1834, New Egypt; 1835-36, Staten Island.
Aug. 26, 1853	Sara Hill Boehm died. "She was a help-meet indeed".
	1857 he took "supernumerary relation" (retirement). We have almost no record of his movements or activities for the next eighteen years. He did attend the General Conference, 1844; when the Southern Methodists withdrew.
Feb. 15, 1856	He spent a two-month period around and in Lancaster City and County. The *Reminiscences* reports some details[10] including a visit and preaching at Boehm's Chapel, Easter Sunday, and ending with a visit at the 1856 Philadelphia Conference.
Jan. 1859	In the *Reminiscences*[11] Henry talks of a visit to Baltimore and to Cincinnati, with some details and nostalgia.

Later 1859-60	"After my return home, I again visited the West and spent a year in Cincinnati".
May 14, 1864	Attended General Conference, at Philadelphia. *Reminiscences* quotes a *Daily Advocate* transcript of his address delivered there.

This is the last chronological information cited in the *Reminiscences*, except, of course, the many details about his centennial-year celebration full report there,[12] which additional pages incorporate the essential and only difference between the two editions of the *Reminiscences* - 1865 and 1875. Let this information be an invitation for readers to obtain these fascinating *Reminiscences* reports! The book, with Index is available from the Boehms Chapel Society.

Bishop Francis Asbury - Henry's Closest Friend

Bishop Francis Asbury, The Prophet Of The Long Road, of the United Methodist Church, fashioned a significant part of that road in his numerous paths through Lancaster County, Pennsylvania, with the Boehms and at historic Boehms Chapel. For one thing, it can be safely reported that it was at Boehm's, that "circuit riding" learned to speak "Dutch".

The depth of Christian love which Henry Boehm expressed throughout his life long time with Bishop Asbury was also very mutually felt by Asbury for all the Boehm's families. He was the first to call Martin "Father Boehm"; to report that traveling circuit riders "found welcome hospitality" at the Boehms households prior to 1770; and to imply that he visited there around 1780, although his first recorded visit is 1783.

Of the fifteen or more published biographies of Francis Asbury, Henry Boehm probably knew Bishop Asbury more intimately and more profoundly than any other person, through his traveling companionship over a longer period than any other companion. Well over half of the text in *Boehm's Reminiscences* deals with Henry's intimate associations with the Bishop. In 1875 Dr. J. B. Wakeley, who helped Henry write his personal Journal Autobiography said: "...Henry gives the best description of Bishop Asbury ever written; and no man ever knew him better..."[13]

It is not surprising, therefore, that a Lancaster

County writer should have caught the vision of the need to see a report on the correlation of the tours and visits of Francis Asbury and Henry Boehm, at the Lancaster County crossroads, where Henry was born and where Asbury's work is perhaps most typically illustrated -- using Asbury's *Journal* and Henry Boehm's *Reminiscences* as major sources.[14]

It seems appropriate to compile this separate listing of dates and events, although some of these references appear elsewhere in this history. And it is my hope that the Heiges article will be published in full, in some popular pamphlet form, in the widest possible distribution. It deserves to be reprinted.

The first recorded visit of Francis Asbury to Martin Boehm's home in Lancaster county was July 31, 1783. The next time he was a bishop! He visited here again twenty more times, the last being nine months before his death March 31, 1816. The following is a brief recording of the dates and at least one excerpt of a prominent occurrence for each visit.

July 31- Aug. 4, 1783	Preached at Martin Boehm's house. Asbury: "This is a barren land to religion, yet fruitful in everything else".
July 10, 1789	Asbury also called on several Lancaster County clergymen.
Sept. 28, 1791	Asbury's first sermon at Boehm's Chapel.
July 3-6, 1792	Asbury: "...rode to our old brother Martin Boehm...preached there".
July 26- Aug. 3, 1799	Asbury: "Martin Boehm is all upon springs and wings, since the Lord blessed his grandchildren. His son Henry is greatly led out in public exercises".
Aug. 23-25, 1800	Asbury: "Our Dutch, German Methodists are as kind and more lively than many of the American ones".
July 22-25, 1803	Henry Boehm's first (short) visit on tour with Bishop Asbury.
July 25-28, 1804	The annual session of the Philadelphia annual Conference was held at Soudersburg, Lancaster County.
Aug. 8-12, 1805	Asbury: "Lancaster is still unpropitious to Methodism".
Aug. 23-25, 1807	This year records the Methodist

	gathering in Lancaster. The Methodist Discipline was first translated into English, at Lancaster, with Henry Boehm as the facilitator.
June 8, 1808	Henry Boehm is now Bishop Francis Asbury's fulltime "traveling companion".
March 30, 1809	Henry: "Bishop Asbury and my father never met without a thrill of delight".
July 28-29, 1809	Asbury: "Delightful rest at Martin Boehm's".
Aug. 3-6, 1810	The start of their third tour out through the West and South.
April 5, 1811	Bishop McKendree preached at Boehm's Chapel.
Aug. 9-19, 1811	(Following their first tour through Canada) Asbury's sermon at Boehm's Chapel was Martin's last to hear him preaching. Asbury's longest stay at Boehm's.
April 3-9, 1812	Martin's death hastened their return. Asbury's sermon at his funeral service at Boehm's, April 5th.
Aug. 11-17, 1812	Henry ends traveling with Asbury. Asbury: "For five years he has been my constant companion. He served me as a son; he served me as a brother; he served me as a servant; he served me as a slave".
April 3, 1813	Asbury: "At mother Boehm's. Preached at Boehm's Chapel".
July 31- Aug. 10, 1813	During this, also, longer visit, Asbury wrote his famous "Valedictory Statement" while at Martin Boehm's house.
June 27-29, 1915	Asbury's last visit to Lancaster County. (Note: parting scenes, at Lancaster with Henry.) Asbury: "And how the new bridge stretches its pride the length across the wide Susquehanna...Columbia bridge is surely a noble work".

Hopefully all readers will be able to see and read the full text of George Heiges' published work on *Asbury and Boehm In Lancaster County*. It is a significant and thoroughly researched and documented, factual historic report. For example, it details Henry's visit to Lancaster County in old age, including the reference to his visit, at age 94, July 1868, attending the National Methodist Campmeeting Association, meeting at Manheim.

Along with Heiges' material, this significant Manheim gathering should also be reported in full, when the History Of Lancaster County Methodism is published. It also appeared first in a publication of the Lancaster County Historical Society bulletin. It deserves to be reprinted and widely distributed.[15]

CHAPTER 3

HAIL, BOEHMS CHAPEL

The Early Beginnings

The earlier 1943 edition as introduction, talked about when Methodism first came to Lancaster County and suggested 1775, quoting Henry Boehm, who said a "Class was formed at my father's house that year; and that my mother, who joined then, belonged to the first race of Methodists in America".[16]

That subject: "The Coming of Methodism" holds great interest for many, and especially when it asks "How?" and "When?" For example, the Methodist Episcopal Church, general Conference of 1912 enacted a resolution "...the time and place of the origin of American Methodism is in dispute, between Sam's Creek (Maryland) and New York (City)...appointed a study commission...to determine if possible whether the priority belongs to Maryland (Strawbridge's Society) or to New York (Embury's Society)."[17]

However, our interest here is simply to identify some of the people and if possible some early, first dates, in order to get a feeling for the developments, and how the Boehm's area related to the movement which was taking place.

John Wesley is church history's founder of Methodism. By Methodism we mean the religious "Great Awakening" combining emphases on personal religious experience and spiritually motivated serious social change. Pursuing this mission, the object is to see "holiness" of faith and life spread throughout the nations, and thus to fulfill the biblical and especially the New Testament requirements for religious faithfulness.

The central issue was winning souls and making converts. To systematize the preaching and help spread the Methodist message throughout the colonial areas became the urgent priority. The first written request from America for such help came in 1768. By 1770 there were at least seven Methodist preachers in America, with more to come. Francis Asbury arrived 1771.

But one of the most important features of the system was that John Wesley was finding ways successfully to enlist and train committed lay leaders, to preach and to organize local Societies. And even before he could arrange to send missionaries to America, some of the "local preachers" (laymen) were among the first to respond in leadership, spreading the gospel here.

Lancaster City area, though on a thoroughfare along the major routes from areas of Philadelphia and Baltimore, early centers of settled Methodist Societies, Henry Boehm later reported the first two efforts at Lancaster had failed, "it was very hard soil for Methodism."[18] Joseph Pilmoor preached the first Methodist sermon at Lancaster, passing through the city as an itinerant, June 1772; although a Class was not formed in the city until about 1805 and First Methodist Church grounded 1807-09.

In contrast to that "hard soil" the country area around the Boehms' farm was more fertile for early Methodism, in the Lancaster County area. Martin Boehm and his wife had a significant series of Wesleyan-style religious awakenings. Martin experienced "conversion" and "newbirth"; selection by his Mennonite congregation in ordination to be a minister; and in a short time selection as a bishop - all before 1770.

When the first Methodist itinerant preachers went forward from Philadelphia and Baltimore areas they were warmly welcomed at Boehms. The Boehm families knew what the Methodist preachers were talking about! And the several Boehms' families at the old homestead became "places of hospitality" and later renowned preaching places.

It is believed that Robert Strawbridge of the Baltimore area was the first itinerant Methodist to preach at Boehms, probably prior to 1770. Henry Boehm, writing about that period, later, recalled the names of seventeen Methodist fathers who "found their way into the rural districts of Lancaster County, Pa." and "from whom I heard the Gospel and to whom I am indebted for my Methodism...pioneers who introduced Methodism into Lancaster County.[19]

We will now turn again to the 1891 *Methodist Messenger* newspaper and the pastor of Boehm's Chapel at that time, for his description, to use the paper's headline, of

Methodist Preaching at Boehm's

This September centennial-year, 1891, issue of the *Methodist Messenger* carries three long articles about Boehms. The first, written by the pastor, C. S. Mervine, makes reference to some of the earliest preachers and evaluates some aspects of their ministry. It includes a lot of factual information in its history.

At the foot of the hill on which Boehm's Chapel stands there was built about the middle of the 18th century a house, which before many years became a renowned preaching place. It was built by Martin Boehm, on the farm where he was born, and where his father, Jacob Boehm, resided until his death in 1780, in the 87th year of his age. Jacob Boehm was the grandfather of the Rev. Henry Boehm, through whose labors Methodism became permanently established in many parts of Lancaster County.

In 1756 Martin Boehm was called to the ministry among the people called Mennonites, and his house became a place for the public worship of God.

To this place, as well as to every place open to them, the early Methodist preachers came and found a hearty welcome, for Martin Boehm was earnest in his purpose to advance the image of Christ and was ready to open the way for all who came in Christ's name as bearers of joyful tidings.

To this house came Robert Strawbridge, an earnest Christian, who, although disregarding the demands made by some of his brethren in respect to the administration of the sacraments, did much good by his faithful presentation of the truth, and led many out of chains into the liberty of the Gospel. Also, in this house Richard Webster and William Thomas were accustomed to preach.

Here Benjamin Abbott, one of the wonders of America, an innocent, holy man, a living exponent of sanctification, came, and aroused the people by his mighty thunderings. This wonderful man had left a description of the scene on one occasion of his preaching. "At Boehm's we found a large congregation. When I came to my application, the

Boehm's Chapel as it looked in 1791

Boehms Chapel, 1791. Twenty years after the Methodist Circuit Riders started to visit the Boehm's residence, as "riders for the Gospel," the Chapel was erected on the hill. (See the description of this, first photograph, from which the sketch was made on Notes No. 20) power of the Lord came in such a manner that the people fell all about the house, and their cries might be heard afar off. This alarmed the wicked, who sprang for the doors in such haste that they fell over one another."

"The cry of mourners was so great that I thought to give out a hymn to drown the noise, and desired one of our English friends to raise it; but as soon as he began to sing the power of the Lord struck him, and he pitched under the table, and there lay like a dead man. I gave it out again, and asked another to raise it. As soon as he attempted he fell also. I then made the third attempt, and the power of the Lord came upon me in such a manner that I cried out, and was amazed. I then saw that I was fighting against God, and did not attempt to sing again".

Mr. Boehm, the owner of the house, and a preacher among the Germans, cried out, "I never saw God in this way before". "Tis, be sure", said he, clapping his hands, "a pentecost, be sure".

"Prayer was all through the house, upstairs and down. A watch-night having been appointed for that evening and seeing no prospect for this meeting being over, although it had begun at eleven o'clock, I told Mr. Boehm we had better quietly withdraw from the meeting-house."

"I consulted with Mr. Boehm who should preach in the evening. We had a very large congregation in the evening, to whom one of the German preachers preached. Then Mr. Boehm gave an exhortation in the German language, and after him a young man gave a warm exhortation in the same tongue. Then I arose and hardly knew how to speak, there had been so much said and it was now growing late. However, I spoke, and the Lord laid to his helping hand as he had done in the day time. Divers fled, and made their way out of the house, and then it appeared as if there were none left but what were earnestly engaged in prayer; some praising God, and others crying for mercy. I told Mr. Boehm that I should not be fit for the duties of the ensuing day if I did not retire, so we went to the house about twelve o'clock and took some refreshments and went to bed. In the morning I found the people were still engaged, and had been all night."

Sylvester Hutchinson, another Son of Thunder, came to this house in 1790 and aroused the community, and a glorious revival of religion followed.

Richard Whatcoat, then a Presiding Elder and afterward a bishop, was at this revival and furnished to the people the plan for the Chapel, which was built on Boehm's farm, the deed being executed by Jacob Boehm, the son of Martin, and his successor in the ownership of the farm. Here came the preachers, always sure of a welcome. Here came the Bishops on their visits to the Conferences. After a time the Circuit preachers came regularly to Boehm's, and many glorious seasons were enjoyed by them and the people to whom they ministered.

A remarkable season of refreshing was a quarterly meeting held in 1798. Thomas Ware was Presiding Elder, and William Colbert and William P. Chandler were the preachers on the circuit.

The meeting began on Saturday, and while the presiding elder was praying, the Holy Ghost filled the house where they were assembled. The work of revival commenced, and such were the cries of distress, the prayers for mercy heard all over the house that it was impossible for Mr. Ware to preach.

At this quarterly meeting Henry Boehm was wonderfully blessed. He declares: "There God restored to me the joy of his salvation. Then I united with the Church, a duty I ought to have performed years before."

Concerning this quarterly Meeting the Mss. Journal of the Rev. William Colbert records, under date of March 10, 1798: "Saturday, 10, at the Quarterly meeting at the meeting house near Martin Boehm's, Brother Ware consulted with Brother Chandler and myself, on, whether we should have, but one, or two sermons to-day. We told him to preach, and we would preach or exhort as we felt ourselves at liberty; but instead of two sermons, or one sermon, we had none, but something that was far better - sinners crying for mercy all over the house, below and in the galleries, and a goodly number brought to rejoice in a sense of their acceptance with God. At night there was also a considerable move among the people." The Rev. Thomas Ware said that this condition of things continued "all that day and night, and indeed for the greater part of three days". - J. S. J. McConnell.

Francis Asbury, our Pioneer Bishop, and the Rev. Jesse Lee, the founder of Methodism in New England and the early historian of American Methodism, were together at Boehm's in 1799.

Bishop Asbury's first visit to Martin Boehm's was made in 1783, and nearly every year thereafter he found there a resting place for a few days, "where he answered letters, and refitted for his long journeys to the West and South."

Soudersburg Methodist Church -- built 1801. Located at 2948 Route 30, East, this old former church building (now a residence) stands along Route 30, east. In 1865 Henry wrote of it, "...The Philadelphia Conference of 1804 was held here, May 28. Methodism was introduced here in 1801. The Conference was held in a private room, at the house of Benjamin Souders, that the meeting house might be used for preaching. There were 120 preachers present...the influence of the Conference was beneficial in all that region. My soul exulted at the idea of a Methodist Conference in my native county." (Rem. p. 113) Photo is courtesy of Lancaster County Historical Society.

Bishop Asbury's last visit to Boehm's was in June, 1815. Under date of June 30th, he has recorded: "Happy at Mother Boehm's. A pleasing providence according to my wishes had brought Henry in a few moments before us".

We might go over the records of the Conference and tell of the eighty or more preachers who have been connected with Boehm's as either preacher in charge or as junior preacher, but alas! for us, we can record but little more than their names. They are gone, and the "records of their deeds, would'st thou know; go search the records of heaven," for on earth but little is recorded of them. Concerning their privations, their journeyings and their sufferings we know but little. Two tombstones in the grave yard attached to Boehm's Chapel testify of the early death of Michael H. R. Wilson and Will Jessop, the latter saying, as he died "My work is done, Glory! Glory!"

The flight of time soon brought round the year 1840. What changes! The Methodist families have removed, and last of all John Boehm, the son of Martin, has removed to Lancaster, and the Church is left to the tender mercies of those who despised Methodism. John Boehm had left a tenant on his farm, who did not like to entertain Methodist preachers, even though a room had been reserved for them, and special agreement made to care for them. The preachers had nowhere to go nearer than McAlister's, at Conestoga, or to Strasburg.

A preacher yet living "in age and feebleness extreme", writes thus: "At the time I was placed in charge of the Strasburg circuit, I found Boehm's in a very low state; we had preaching every other Sunday, but when John Boehm removed, there was no one left that took interest in the Church, and as there were other points where I was greatly needed, I was compelled to take the Master's work at the other appointments."

For about 15 years there was only an occasional service held at Boehm's although the few scattered members still existed as a class.

In 1856, there was a grand revival at Conestoga Centre, which brought the Church at that point into existence, and stimulated hope to the remnant at Boehm's. Rev. Daniel Rinier and F. M. Brady, local preachers from Conestoga, came to Boehm's, and a glorious revival resulted. An incident will show the spirit that existed at that time.

When Bro. Rinier had finished his day's work in the stone quarry, he would change his clothes and walk five

miles to Boehm's to preach. His wife thought to stop this, and on one occasion put out of his reach a clean white shirt, but Amos McAlister, a near neighbor, came to the rescue, and furnished the clean attire. Under the stress of this persecution, Brother Rinier received of God such an outpouring of his spirit that he became eloquent, persuasive and energetic, for with a bound he descended from the lofty pulpit and called sinners to the altar, and a large number came immediately; the only time flame of revival fire spread throughout the neighborhood, and the Church became again a power for good. Many who were converted at that time yet remain among us, but many others have gone to their heavenly home.

The church was then joined with Safe Harbor, and the pastor who took charge is yet living, and will be present at our Centennial celebration.

The 1891 article by pastor C. S. Mervine also printed a picture of the chapel, and at the end an explanation of the picture's source was given, important to us here because it is the only, earliest picture of the chapel.

It says: **The picture from which our cut of Boehm's Chapel was made, we are indebted to Mr. George M. Steinman, of Lancaster, who kindly had a copy made from a picture in his possession. The cut represents the Chapel as it appeared prior to its complete reformation and internal improvement in 1883. The windows on the sides were then enlarged, while those over the entrance were walled up. In the rear gable, however, the window which was opened from the pulpit was allowed to remain, so that a visitor to the historic place can form an estimate of the height from which the fathers looked upon the saints and sinners to whom they preached the gospel.**

I remember being able to borrow that very same, old-fashioned printer's cut, at the Lancaster Newspaper Library, which I also used in printing a reproduction of the Chapel, in the 1943 writing. This George M. Steinman was founder of Steinman Hardware Co., Lancaster.[20]

A Running Account

Following that rather long introduction, from a former 19th century pastor at Boehms, we turn to some other sources and a body of information also about the developing historic movement around this ancient shrine. (Note: In this "running account" of the emerging history of Boehms Chapel several composition forms should be observed: One, the name of the conference-appointed "pastor-in-charge" and his date of ministry is included in these columns only when some historic information or some anecdote about that period is printed here. Otherwise, the year-sequence depicted is not cited in the text; and in that case the pastor's name appears only in the listing at Appendix A. Two, throughout this section reference is sometimes made to details and information written elsewhere. To minimize writing duplication, readers should anticipate such in-copy references.)

In The Very Beginning

1775. The first piece of ground owned by Methodists in Lancaster County was about one acre given by Jacob Boehm, largely through the influence of its one-time owner, his father, Martin Boehm. A copy of the original deed showing the property transfer is displayed on the wall at Boehms United Methodist Church.

And here the first Methodist chapel was built in Lancaster County. The first Methodist Class, as early as 1775 met at Boehm's house; and if more space were needed, as was the custom in the area, meetings gathered in the barn of the old Boehm's homestead. (The saga of the "church in the house" cf: I Cor. 16:19 is most reassuring!)

At this early date, the Elder (District Superintendent) also traveled as a station preacher as well as through the District. Districts were large, like unto our "Areas" today, and included many "circuits" by today's usage. The "elders" and "circuit riders" who tried to cover the large Eastern Pennsylvania area of which Boehm's home was a preaching point, are listed from the very beginning in the first Conference Minutes, at the archives and history center at St. George's Church, Philadelphia.

1788. The date for the start of the Philadelphia Annual Conference is 1788, although it is "officially" dated 1802. Boehm's Church is included in the earliest records, always a part of a circuit, variously named Chester, Lancaster, Strasburg, Safe Harbor, etc., and not called "Boehms Circuit" until 1889.

1791. The names in the Clergy List Appendix seem clear for the first sixteen years, though surprisingly there is no special news from or about any particular circuit rider's role in relation to the construction of

Boehm's Chapel, 1791; except perhaps Elder John McClosky whom Henry's journal cites twelve times, characteristically: "and others, to whom I am indebted for my Methodism."[21] The explanation is, obviously, that the Boehm's people were taking the responsibility for the new building initiatives, in the pastor's absence!

1795. In the year 1795 William Jessop died in Strasburg, at the home of John Miller, also a family of great friends of the early preachers. Henry says he knew Jessop intimately and heard him preach often. With Asbury preaching (as Jessop requested) his funeral and burial were at Boehms. At this writing, a proposal is before the Boehms Chapel Society that his old grave site be selected to receive the (new) Methodist Clergy Gravemarker, at ceremonies in June, 1991.

When Jesse Lee visited Boehm's in 1799 he said, "...I then went and took a view of the grave of William Jessop, who was buried at the meeting house three or four years ago. He was a favorite friend of mine and a traveling preacher for many years. I felt very solemn when I thought of his departure. I understand that he departed this life in the full triumph of faith. His last words were, my work is done, Glory! Glory! and so died away. O Lord, let me die the death of the righteous".

1796. In 1796 the Strasburg Circuit is first mentioned, combining the Chester and Lancaster Circuits. Why didn't they call it Boehm's? Apparently the historicity and significance attached to the Boehm's location today was not similarly realized in its first decade! Also in 1797, the term "Presiding Elder" was first coined and used officially in our Conference.

1799. The reference above, taken from Thrift's Memoir of Rev. Jesse Lee also tells about that 1799 visit. "At Boehm's meeting house I preached on Isa. 31:21 and had a precious season, in preaching and the power of the Lord was with us; and there were tears shed by the hearers. Thank God for another happy meeting. Bishop Asbury preached...and gave us a good discourse".

This August, 1799 visit of Asbury's was the occasion when he wrote, "Martin Boehm is all upon wings and springs since the Lord has blessed his grandchildren; his son Henry is greatly led out in public exercises".

1800. You recall, it is said that Bishop Whatcoat proposed the design for Boehms Chapel. On Sunday, August 23, 1800 he preached there. With Asbury they had ridden 170 miles during the preceding week and were lodging at

Bishop Francis Asbury. The history of this popular image of Francis Asbury is unknown. (The print for this reproduction was made by Don Eckert Studios, Lancaster.)

the home of Martin Boehm's son-in-law Abraham Keaggy. Asbury wrote, "Our Dutch Methodists are as kind and more lively than many of the American ones".

1802. 1802 is a banner year also. Henry Boehm was received on trial by the Methodist Episcopal Church. The historic location of early Methodism, the Soudersburg Church, was built this year. The "Philadelphia Conference" is mentioned in the Minutes, officially as such. See the old picture of Soudersburg, and note the reference to it in the Appendix on Lancaster County Landmarks.

1803. The next year also, Asbury is in Lancaster County, being accompanied on a "trial" basis by Henry Boehm who is now doing some "experimental" preaching in German while with the Bishop, as an important transition to his fulltime traveling companionship.

1804. Sunday, May 27, 1804, Bishop Asbury "crossed the Susquehanna River at McCalls Ferry and came to Martin Boehm's, and after preaching in the Chapel rode on to Soudersburg." With one hundred and twenty five preachers present, this was the first Methodist Annual Conference held in Lancaster County. Henry Boehm has written a full account of the Conference and rejoicingly says, "My soul exulted at the idea of a Methodist Conference in my native county; it was an era in the history of Methodism in that region...the Conference lasted five days, during which the Bishop preached twice..."[22]

1807. In the year 1807, the first church building at Strasburg was erected. This Society and the Boehm's group had many, continuing relationships, as a close neighbor and fellow-circuit church, with many of the same families in each, walking often and riding to each other's meetings. This was the year, too, when Henry "...received a letter from Bishop Asbury requesting me to meet him at my father's, which I did".

Henry As Asbury's Companion

1808. Presumably, Asbury wanted to talk with Henry and his family about his next appointment! The 1808 Conference Minutes read "Henry Boehm travels with Bishop Asbury". Henry says of it, **This year was an era in my ministerial life. I was no longer confined to a small diocese. Though my name in the Minutes for 1808 stands as Pennsylvania missionary, I was there only a few weeks previous to the General Conference; the rest of the year**

I was traveling with Bishop Asbury.

My new field of labor was a splendid school for a young minister, and he must have been a dull scholar that did not learn important lessons. It enlarged my knowledge of the country, of the Church, and of her ministers....Asbury was sixty-three years when I began to travel with him...he was feeble and suffered from many infirmities...

"By agreement I was to meet the bishop at Perry Hall, Md., June 5th...and then we were to proceed on our Western tour. I took leave of my aged mother with tears, and my father accompanied me for some distance. On our way we came to a Campmeeting...Jesse Lee (there) in all his glory preached three powerful sermons...and a most affecting parting with my father...he loved me as Jacob did Joseph...not there at the time, I supposed the bishop would wait 'til I arrived...but I found he had left the day before...he never waited for any man, and wanted no man to wait for him...His motto was 'The King's business requires haste!'[23] So Henry misses the Bishop for his first appointment!

1809. 1809 marks when First Church, Lancaster was dedicated, and the Lancaster Circuit designated. It was part of the Schuylkill District, including all the area between Dauphin in Pennsylvania and Wilmington in Delaware, between the Susquehanna and Schuylkill rivers. Henry Boehm presided over this District and Circuit for about fifteen years including, of course, Boehm's Chapel.

1810. Henry's 1810 record of a visit home, after the annual round through the conferences is quite revealing. "After unparalleled toil and suffering we reached Middletown, PA...took dinner with our old friend...the neighbors heard of our arrival and urged (the bishop) to preach...but he had only time to pray with them...but it was very refreshing, after having for so long put up at miserable taverns and among strangers...we journeyed on to my father's...I felt 'there is no place like home'...that day we rode fifty miles...we had traveled two thousand two hundred and twenty-five miles...the bishop preached on Saturday evening at Boehm's Chapel...his letters were generally sent to the care of my father...fifteen letters...he answered them all on Saturday."

The Death of Martin Boehm

1812. 1812 marks the death of the old patriarch of Boehms. We record here the details, as reported by Henry in the *Reminiscences*. For its history lessons and for the impact of Henry Boehm's human interest reports, the full record of Henry's account is made here.[24]

A short time before the conference closed at Leesburg Bishop Asbury said to me. "Henry, as soon as conference adjourns you must have the horses ready and we must go right to your father's." I reminded him of appointments he had sent on to Baltimore and through the eastern shore of Maryland. He said, "never mind, we can get them filled; I tell you we must go right to your father's." We were then one hundred miles distant.

The reason of the sudden change in his plans I believed to be, the bishop had presentiment or an impression that my father was dead. How else could we account for his abandoning a long list of appointments, changing his entire route, and hastening on to my father's?

When we reached Samuel Binkley's, who lived a mile from our old homestead, the mystery was solved; there we heard my father was dead. The aged Asbury wept, and I felt sad at the thought I should see him no more. I learned that he was taken sick the 17th of March, and on Monday the 23rd he departed this life in great peace and triumph, so his mournful words proved true that "we should never see each other again."

The bishop makes this record: "Friday, a cold disagreeable ride brought us across the country to Samuel Binkley's; here I received the first intelligence of the death of my dear old friend, Martin Boehm".

The next day, Saturday, we passed by his new made grave to the old homestead, where I found my mother in all the sorrows of widowhood. The bishop writes thus: "Sabbath, April 5, I preached at Boehm's Chapel the funeral sermon of Martin Boehm, and gave my audience some very interesting particulars of his life." His text was, "Behold an Israelite indeed, in whom there is no guile." Immense was the crowd; and the occasion was one of mournful interest. The bishop drew the character of his life-time friend with great exactness, and also that of many of his contemporaries, particularly William Otterbein.

"Martin Boehm", he said, "was plain in dress and manners. When age had stamped its impress of reverence upon him he filled the mind with the noble idea of a patriarch. As the head of a family, a father, a neighbor, a friend, a companion, the prominent feature of his character was goodness; you felt that he was good. His mind was strong, and well stored with the learning necessary for one whose aim is to preach Christ with apostolic zeal and simplicity."

Martin Boehm had frequent and severe conflicts in his own mind, produced by the necessity he felt himself under of offending his Mennonite brethren by the zeal and doctrines of his ministry. Some he gained, but most of them opposed him. He had difficulties also with "The United Brethren". It was late in life that he joined the Methodists, to whom, long before, his wife and children had attached themselves. The head of the house had two societies to pass through to arrive at the Methodists, and his meek and quiet spirit kept him back.

In his ministry he did not make the Gospel a charge to anyone; his award was souls and glory.

The virtue of hospitality was practiced by his family as a matter of course, and in following the impulses of their own generous natures the members of his household obeyed the oft-repeated charge of their head to open his doors to the homeless, that the weary might be solaced and the hungry fed. And what a family was here presented to an observant visitor! Here was order, quiet, occupation.

The father, if not absent on a journey of five hundred miles in cold, hunger, and privation, proclaiming the glad tidings of salvation to his dispersed German brethren, might, by his conduct under his own roof, explain to a careful looker-on the secret of a parent's success in rearing a family to the duties of piety, to the diligent and useful occupation of time, and to the uninterrupted exhibition of reflected and reciprocal love, esteem, and kindness in word and deed.

If it is true, as generally believed, that the mother does much toward forming the character of her children, it will be readily allowed that Martin Boehm had an able help-meet in his pious wife. The offspring of this noble pair have done them honor. The son Jacob, immediately upon his marriage, took upon himself the management of the farm, that his excellent father might, "without carefulness", extend his labors more far and wide.

"A younger son, Henry, is a useful minister of the Methodist connection, having the advantage of being able to preach in English and German. We are willing to hope that the children of Martin Boehm, and his children's children to the third, fourth, and last generations, will have cause to thank God that his house for fifty years has

been a house for the welcome reception of Gospel ministers, and one in which the worship of God has been uninterruptedly preserved and practiced. O ye children and grandchildren! O rising generation, who have so often heard the prayers of this man of God in the houses of your fathers! O ye Germans to whom he has long preached the word of truth! Martin Boehm being dead yet speaketh. O hear his voice from the grave exhorting you to repent, to believe, to obey!"

After the bishop had finished his impressive discourse, which was listened to with tears and sighs by a numerous auditory, he called on me to speak. I endeavored to do so, but when I stood in the pulpit where I had so often beheld my father, in the church that bore his name, with my venerable mother before me, tottering over the grave, my relatives all around me, where I could look out of the window into the burying-ground and see the new-made grave of my father, my eyes filled with tears, and I was so overcome that I could only utter, "Let silence speak".

The people were deeply affected all over the house. There was weeping from many eyes. My father was greatly beloved in life, and deeply lamented in death. I heard the venerable Asbury often when he was great, and he was peculiarly great on funeral occasions, but then he far transcended himself.

He called upon Thomas Ware to make some observations. He had long known and loved my father, and his remarks were very touching and appropriate. The bishop then called upon Abram Keaggy, who had married my sister; but his feelings overcame, and he sat down and wept, and thus we all wept together. A spectator might have said, "Behold how they loved him."

My father was in his eighty-seventh year when he died, and had preached the Gospel fifty-five years.

The Bishop and Henry, notwithstanding the death of father Boehm and the loneliness of the sainted mother, spent only three days at the old homestead. Later that summer they returned, however, and Henry says about it: "We left for my mother's, passing through the valley of Wyoming, and arrived at the old mansion the 11th of August, 1812. Bishop Asbury wept for his old friend, and I for my father."

Henry Boehm - A Presiding Elder

1813. The 1813 Conference appointed Henry Boehm as

a Presiding Elder. It is of significance that he was placed in that position, at once following the end of his successful five-year tour with Bishop Asbury. Henry wrote "Bishop Asbury thought I was needed among the Germans, and that I ought to be near my mother, who was living within the bounds of my Schuylkill District."

Missing, somehow, from the *Reminiscences* record of these years is any reference to his (let's call it) "pastoral work" around Boehm's and whether or not he preached (often) at the chapel. He was living in Philadelphia.

1815. The big account from 1815 is Asbury's last visit at Boehm's. Henry said, "On the fourth of July I was visiting my mother, and had not been there fifteen minutes when, to our great joy, Bishop Asbury unexpectedly arrived....He remained two days. He had visited that old home for thirty-five years...my aged mother and the bishop bade one another adieu for the last time. I went with him to Lancaster, and then was reluctant to leave him, and so I went a little further, for I had an impression that I should see his face no more."

"He gave me such excellent advice, and cautioned me to take good care of my health...He then embraced me in his arms, pressed me to his bosom, gave me his last kiss and benediction. He rode on while I lingered and gazed till his venerable form was beyond my vision. I felt a veneration for Bishop Asbury I never had for any other human being, and I loved him as I loved my own dear father."

In searching for the location of this historic farewell, we discovered that the late John B. Good, Esquire, of Lancaster had once recorded "I heard from the lips of the Rev. Henry Boehm that this parting scene occurred at the corner of West King and Charlotte Streets, Lancaster, where the Plow Tavern then stood..."

This event is of special interest to present day UMC historians. The significance of this Historic Farewell Scene was selected as one of eight locations to be included in a UMC Lancaster County Roadside Markers Project in 1984.[25] The committee labored over two things: the most representative location, and also a property owner's permission. Two churches were approached: the Lutheran Church (at West King and Charlotte Sts.) and the Covenant United Methodist Church (at West Orange near Charlotte Sts.). Both churches refused to give permission for the marker's location. But the owner of the George

Lyter Insurance Agency (corner of West End Avenue and Columbia Avenue) did gladly oblige and the marker stands attached on the corner of that building.

Henry As Pastor Of His Home Church

1822. In 1822 Henry Boehm was appointed to the Lancaster circuit which, of course, includes Boehm's, and Joseph Holdich was his associate.[26] It suggests a fine personal touch on the part of the conference that Henry should now have been preaching again at his home circuit, when also his mother was in her last days. She died in November of that year. She is buried beside his father at Boehm's cemetery.

1824. 1824 is to be remembered as a year calling attention to church records. As readers know, unfortunately we have no early records of membership or church administration from Boehms.[27] But on the circuit, the Safe Harbor Church's 1865 membership records, show its oldest member Jacob Steiner was received in 1824, when James Moore was pastor at Boehms. References will be made to the active, 1865 years of pastor J.E. Keesler, whose membership records show the 1824 date.

1825. In 1825 Boehm's was transferred to the Strasburg Circuit, and the Conference changed the district name to Philadelphia District. And in 1831 the circuit name was changed/recorded as "Strasburg and Columbia". There is still no sure way to know of the vitality at Boehms, but in a Strasburg 1895 Centennial program at the (circuit) a Strasburg Church revival "revived the entire community; there were 347 conversions on the circuit, most of them at Strasburg...the revival made a wondrous stir in the entire neighborhood, many persons attended from Boehms, Old Road, Soudersburg, and other places six or eight miles distance."

1835. For a ten-year period only two small bits of information appear, in addition to the pastors' names. 1835 shows a new "station" in the Minutes, "Susquehanna Mission" presumed to be the first organized work at Safe Harbor. And a membership record, similar to that cited above, where one A. W. Kauffman, received into full connection in 1840, is of interest to United Brethren in Christ Church reporting, for under remarks, "he withdrew Feb., 1866, for purposes of preaching among the United Brethren".

CHAPTER 4

FIRST LOVE LOST

By 1840 it is considered Methodism was at a lower state around Boehms. Attrition changes had come to some families. Son, John Boehm had moved from the farm to Lancaster. A tenant farmer had no interest in Methodist preachers, even a room traditionally reserved for them at Boehm's was no longer available, according to a story told by a former pastor.

We are talking about a fifteen-year period which, though again attendance and membership records do not exist, the implied reports and suggestions indicate decline. The Strasburg Record does report memberships on the circuit as smaller also in the geographical area, with only five stations: Strasburg, 140; Soudersburg, 49; Enterprise, 30; Georgetown, 60; Boehms, 35.

But the most telling report about the period perhaps are remarks made by Rev. J. B. McCullough, when he attended the centennial in 1891, he related some of his experiences on the circuit in 1847. Quoting from his journal made at Boehms, "The people are much like real heathen. They come in church with their hats on and cigars in their mouths; their conduct was rude and interrupted the services."

(This may have been the time also, according to stories passed on in my hearing in 1943, there was at least one time when a horseman rode into the church services. Another that a misbehaved young man spat tobacco juice down unto the top of bald heads in the congregation.)

McCullough attributed this to the fact that "they did not have preaching for a while. And he noted as he returned time and again the people became more attentive and reverent."

The Period of Renewal

1856 marks a recorded, first turning point in the history of Boehms. Boehms is Lancaster County's first Methodist Church and the mother of Methodist influence here; but now her one daughter is coming to her rescue. In 1856 there was a great revival at Conestoga. It brought the church at that village into existence, and it renewed hope in the remnant at Boehms.

Two local preachers, blessed and inspired by the Conestoga Revival and growing up there, Daniel Rineer and F. M. Brady, came to Boehms and held meetings there. A significant renewal and revival resulted. Both were still remembered when I was writing in 1943. Favorite sons at Conestoga, Daniel Rineer was a "local preacher" and F. M. Brady later became a minister in our local Conference; and he was one of the "surviving preachers" in that list, present for the 1891 bicentennial; and both preached during that week of special services (see below).

A Daniel Rineer incident, from this period and movement, is worth repeating. When he would finish his day's work in the stone quarry, he would change his clothes and walk five miles to Boehms to preach. His wife sought to stop it, and on one occasion put out of his reach a clean white shirt; but Amos McAlister, a near neighbor, came to the rescue, and furnished the clean attire.

The community testifies of favorite son, Daniel Rineer, being led by God's Spirit; of his eloquence and persuasive preaching and power in prayer; and on one occasion his descent from the lofty pulpit at Boehms, calling penitents to the altar, and a large number converted. So, "the flame of revival fire spread throughout the neighborhood, and the Church at Boehms became again a power of good." (Amos McAlister was also among those who testified at the 1891 centennial (see below).

As its developing industry and phenomenal population growth arose, the need grew there for a church at Safe Harbor, after the class had been formed and house meetings were no longer adequate. The circuit was then changed to "Safe Harbor" and Boehm's was joined there in 1856. The pastor, Wm. Major, talked about it in 1891 and his phrase is a telling one. He spoke of the "*reopening*" of Boehm's

Chapel in 1856-71. (See below.)

The pastorate of J. E. Kessler, 1867-1869, should be noted. We now have him to thank for significant record keeping and observe too his records are the only, earliest in existence.[28] According to these records, 255 members were received on "probation" during his three-years on the circuit. No wonder he opened a record book! 51 were received at Boehms. During his years, surely every family must have been influenced by his leadership from Washington Boro to Willow Street, for the circuit then included Boehms, Marticville, Conestoga Center, Safe Harbor, Millersville, Washington Boro.

"Classes" were formed in all these places. (The two precious, old record books including these Class names and attendance, 1866-1888; and a book of "Minutes of the Safe Harbor Circuit Quarterly Conference", 1852-1868, surely cause us to weep because they are the only earliest church records in existence.)

The classes were led by lay members from the churches. Some of them had just been converted in recent revivals, and soon thereupon became class leaders. The names of these leaders at Boehms from this period until 1882 include: Henry H. Hess, Benjamin Stetler, Samuel F. Gall, Marris Hackman, Henry Goss, Abraham Breneman.

Henry Boehm, old and retired, but very interested and interesting was around Lancaster County in these years! A most fascinating entry in one line of Safe Harbor's oldest book, Aug. 4, 1867, records the baptism of Benjamin K. Maynard, adult, by sprinkling, the officiating minister: "Rev. Henry Boehm, aged 92 years." (!)

And in the Marriage Record section of that same old book, July 23, 1868, Henry Greenwalt and Mary A. Weller of Millersville were married "by Rev. Henry Boehm, at Manheim Campmeeting." These records have likely never been noticed with our prevailing interest before. My 1943 writing says, **the other day I was in Strasburg, inquiring for records and documents concerning this dissertation material. I was introduced to their oldest resident, William Bishop, son of the Rev. William Bishop of our Conference. I found M. Bishop, now a retired farmer, in his room midst papers and books which signify his alertness and agility for a man of 93. He apparently remembers almost everything he ever knew!**

As a youth he was living with his uncle, Mr. Steacy, for his mother had died while he was a child. This was the

Boehms Chapel, 1883. The Chapel was "improved" and "rebuilt" inside, through a preservation-and-use project of the congregation in 1883; and it was the church's meetinghouse until 1899. the background and origin of this beautiful old photo is not known. It was donated to the Boehm's Collection by John Kauffman of Marietta.

stopping place for the visiting preachers, he remembers; as Boehm's was near the chapel. Henry Boehm stayed there overnight in 1867! This is the only time Mr. Bishop (age 17 then) ever saw Henry, but he remembers him well. He was a tall strong looking old man with white hair, not one of which was missing. He was straight as an arrow.[29] (I said, down inside, "I just talked with somebody who once talked face-to-face with Henry Boehm.") The historic records at Strasburg Church also affirm that he was in Strasburg in 1867 and preached there.

Improvements at the Chapel

It was a time of growth at Boehms. Washington Boro and Millersville were now dropped from this circuit. 1882 was the year the annual "Report of the Presiding Elder", a substantial feature now part of the *Conference Minutes*, was begun, and it read for Boehms "A church is needed at Willow Street, and it is very difficult to secure an eligible location. A comfortable and conveniently located parsonage is also a necessity on this circuit. Revival reported at Boehms Chapel."

Sixteen years later the "new church was built. It is of the greatest interest, now, to speculate about that timing. If the congregation at Boehm's had indeed built their anticipated new church when they first talked about it in 1882, sixteen years before they did build to replace the Chapel, then the "destruction" that was wrought to the Chapel in the "repair" and "improvement" work of 1883, would not have taken place! And, consequently, the 1980-90's restoration program could probably have been averted!

1883 was a particularly significant year for old Boehms Chapel. The pastor Rev. A. J. Amthor told the story, at the centennial celebration in 1891. "It was during my pastorate the necessary repairs were made in the church. The gallery was unsafe, the windows were loose from the wall, and the roof had many holes. It was decided that the only way to make the building comfortable was to give it a thorough repairing. The galleries were removed; the old high pulpit was taken out; the roof made new; the ceiling lowered, the windows enlarged, and new benches were made. With all these improvements, the building retains so much of its old character that it is readily recognized as the church of 100 years ago."[30]

In view of all developments, especially the last decade

of decision for restoration, it is of interest to observe my written, expressed attitude and opinion as a rookie, student pastor, fifty years ago. Allow me this personal privilege! I wrote in 1943:

His last sentence sounds like an apology. Improvements? no, rather hurtful changes, which took away the Chapel's antiquity and ancient beauty, leaving a deformity of the original, with deep scars from patch-work. Once there was no ceiling under the rafted roof. Ancient and unique galleries marked its three sides under the roof. The period high pulpit was itself beauty in symbolism. Of course, she was weakened by age. but she could have been strengthened without changing. What a shame to cut her down, especially since they were anticipating a new church building. I think she should be restored. I think someone should endow her for complete restoration and permanent repair."[31]

In 1884, the Presiding Elder reported "Boehms Chapel, around which clusters so much that is familiar with the labors of Bishop Asbury and Henry Boehm has been remodeled and greatly improved, at a cost of $750."

CHAPTER 5

THE FIRST CENTENNIAL CELEBRATION

In 1890, the Conference Minutes stated "It is appointed next year to celebrate the centennial of Boehms Chapel, Lancaster County, Pa. This is the oldest edifice built for Methodist Episcopal services in the Conference and is probably the oldest now standing in the country." Historians and researchers have done a lot about the "oldest" and the "first" in our history, as in all others! But, the First, Centennial Year at Boehms Chapel was celebrated in good order, September 16 to 22. Its report is fascinating!

There is perhaps no better way of presenting the entire picture of the historic Boehm's Centennial Celebration than by the announcements and news coverage reports of plans and proceedings as found in the *Lancaster Intelligencer*.

LANCASTER NEWSPAPER REPORTS

Tuesday, September 8, 1891

Built A Century Ago

The celebration of the centennial of Boehm's Church (Methodist) will begin on September 16 and continue on the following Sunday evening.

Prominent ministers from this and other counties will take part in the five-day encampment. It is expected that many people other than members of the congregation will attend. Thee will certainly be a large crowd there on Sunday, September 20.

Boehm's Chapel as the building was first named because it was built on the land of Martin Boehm in 1791, The Boehms contributing largely to its erection. It became a great center of Methodism, and at quarterly meetings people came from Philadelphia and Maryland, and were addressed by the most distinguished preachers of those days. Martin Boehm's father came from the Palatinate in 1715 and settled in Pequea as a farmer and blacksmith, the first and only blacksmith in that half of the county. Martin Boehm was first a Mennonite preacher, and was active in the organization of "The United Brethren in Christ". Rev. Henry Boehm was first among the Methodists to preach in the German language.

Boehm's meeting house is strongly built of stone, and stands upon a level hilltop overlooking the very picturesque Pequea Valley.

There is a large enclosure for the accommodation of the teams of the worshippers, who used to drive many miles to the services. There was a great deal of zeal and energy about that early Methodist, but the congregation after a time became weak and for ten years services were suspended entirely. In 1847 there was a revival and since then the old meetinghouse has been in regular use. It was so well built that there have been very few repairs, and it is an excellent state of preservation.

The seating capacity is about three hundred, and the large galleries and quaint, uncomfortable old box pews are fine relics of those times of few luxuries and stern simplicity. (Note: This reporter must have been writing from a decade-ago acquaintance. The galleries were removed eight years ago.)

Wednesday, September 16, 1891

Tents and Other Accommodations

The second newspaper release followed eight days later, with two full front-page columns under this sub-head. The members of Boehm's Methodist Church have been arranging for months for a celebration of an event that is of interest not only to members of this church but to all the Methodists of the county and state.It is the centennial of Boehm's and a programme of exercises has been arranged. The sermons will be delivered only by those who have been connected with the church either as pastor or as presiding elder (named below).

All of these preachers mentioned will take part in the exercises, except Rev. Samuel Pencost, J. A. Watson of Chester, and Rev. Ganey Oram of Philadelphia, who are too feeble to get there....

Aside of the church a large tent has been erected to accommodate the throngs expected. The preacher will speak from the window of the old church, and those in the tent can thus hear as well as those in the church.

Accommodations have been provided for those who desire to remain overnight; several tents have been erected close to the church. A large tent where refreshments will be served is in charge of S. F. Gall.

The programme as arranged provides for three sermons each day. The first is at ten o'clock in the morning; the second at 3 in the afternoon; and the third at 7, in the evening. Each of the speakers prior to the sermon will give a short address referring to incidents connected with their pastorate of the church.

Saturday, September 19, 1891

The third newspaper release, three days later, ran with a picture of the chapel. Excerpted here, it said, **an edifice that was erected in Pequea a century ago, in this issue is printed a cut of the old church, whose centennial is now being celebrated...it was for many years a headquarters for the Methodists of Lancaster County...An interesting fact of the centennial is that articles used by Rev. henry Boehm a century ago occupy a prominent place in the church...Tomorrow will be the big day of the centennial...Indications point to an attendance of several thousand.**

Monday, September 1, 1891

Sunday at Boehm's - Several Thousand Attend

On Monday morning the *Intelligencer Journal* said, **Boehm's Church, several miles south of Willow Street, was the objective point of thousands of pilgrims on Sunday. Since the beginning of special services to mark the Hundredth anniversary on Wednesday, there have been large crowds daily, but Sunday's assemblage was the greatest that ever gathered there. The place is too far from the railway for visitors to conveniently go by train and the result was that the teams in use will need that part of** the spacious churchyard not occupied by the worshippers, and on either side of the roadway for several hundred yards each way.

Conveyances were constantly arriving and departing, and this fact makes it difficult to estimate the number of persons attending but at least there were between four and six thousand. There were some that drove from the extreme southern portion of the county, and all sections were represented. The toll gate keeper reports that nearly a hundred wagon loads of people from the city attended. The unpiked roads were terribly cut up by the vehicles. Dust was half a foot in depth. The sun was warm but people complained more of dust than the heat.

On the north end of the church a large tent is placed to shelter the crowds, there being no trees near. The benches used in the church are arranged in circles under the canvas and at the east side of the church. The seating capacity was far inadequate. When preaching was in progress those standing densely packed the space not occupied by teams. The speaker's stand is at the corner of the building, and the sermons and prayers were distinctly heard by the vast throng.

Rev. Dr. T. B. Neely of Philadelphia who is well known in the lower end of the county and who preached some of the best sermons at the recent campmeeting at Rawlinsville, officiated at the morning service, which began at 10:30. His discourse was much appreciated. The afternoon sermon was delivered by Rev. D. J. J. McConnell, of the First M. E. Church of the city. A chorus of "Amens!" frequently punctuated his remarks, some of the old-fashioned Methodists in the audience taking this method of showing their approval of what was said. Others were compelled to shed tears, and in fact all must have been affected by his eloquence.

Another sermon of the soul-stirring kind was that of Rev. William L. Gray, corresponding secretary of the Methodist Episcopal Tract Society, Philadelphia. He began at 7:30 and spoke for nearly an hour making frequent appeals for sinners to repent. After prayers were held and a number professed conversion the services of the day ended.

Rev. C. S. Mervine, pastor of the church, announced at the beginning of the afternoon service that a member, who resided a quarter of a mile from the church, was ill. She had a couch placed on the porch of her home and occupied it part of the day, expecting to hear the songs. That she

might enjoy the music Rev. Mervine suggested that extraordinary effort be made by the singers. His remarks inspired them, for a mighty chorus followed.

The centennial services closed on Tuesday evening. Rev. F. M. Brady preached at 8 p.m. today. At 7 p.m. Rev. J. C. Wilson occupied the pulpit. The last sermon will probably be by Rev. Mervine, and Rev. George Cummings of Philadelphia is announced to officiate on Tuesday afternoon at 3 o'clock.

There is expected to be a great revival at Boehm's church this autumn. Congregation and pastor are working in harmony, and churchmen think the impressions made by the centennial sermons will lead many to the altar.

LANCASTER'S METHODIST MESSENGER

Appropriate notice needs to be taken here of *The Methodist Messenger*, a denominational newsletter published in Lancaster, which devoted its September and October issues, 1891, almost exclusively to Boehm's!

Copies of this fascinating tabloid were discovered in the archives at Drew University library. Apparently no copies were systematically preserved in Methodist archives at either Lancaster or Philadelphia. Although several pages of the September issue - showing the picture of the Chapel and some text about the 1891 centennial have been discovered, locally, *viz*: a Boehm's Family member living in Philadelphia has shown off a xerox copy of this page; also the same *Messenger* issue was found among some papers at the Conestoga Methodist Church parsonage, and has been xeroxed there.[33]

The *Methodist Messenger* was the creation/production of two Lancaster Methodist pastors, J. S. J. McConnell of First Methodist Church and C. L. Gaul of St. Paul's Methodist. (The paper staff box designates the first as president, and the second as secretary. It was said to be published monthly. Its subscription price is "ten cents, to the close of the present volume, or January 1st 1892." It was printed by the *Lancaster New Era* newspaper, and it solicited classified ads. The *New Era* bought an ad which read, in part, "...the *Methodist Messenger* is a fair specimen of our newspaper work.")

We can find only five monthly issues, and it appears that the *Messenger* was published only June thru October, 1891. We wonder why it was discontinued, and whether subscribers did indeed receive a rebate, since apparently it did not continue into January. McConnell successfully published a history of First Church in 1893. One would assume and expect to find some reference to the *Messenger* in that history, since he was author of one and president of the other. It is a real puzzler to ask why he did not mention the five-month's history of the *Messenger*. (Xeroxed duplicates of these five issues have been obtained from Drew University library,[34] and have been deposited in the archives room at First UMC, Lancaster.)

The September issue of the *Messenger* explained to its readers why so much space is occupied with matters relating to Boehm's Chapel. "The justification for this is the fact that the centennial of the founding of the Chapel is to be observed during the month of September. We are sure that if our readers are one-half as deeply interested in the story of Martin Boehm and the religious movement that centered at his home one hundred years ago, as we were in preparing the articles which appear in our columns, they will conclude that even more space might be given without detracting from the importance of any other interest at this time. We hope the contemplated celebration may prove an inspiration to the present membership at Boehm's".

Obviously, as implied, the *Messenger* and the Lancaster newspapers are major sources of detailed reporting from Boehm's Centennial. (We have no printed bulletins or brochures from the church.) Note also, the other Lancaster newspaper, the *New Era*, carried one, major story on the Boehm's anniversary. It wrote a full page summary of every detail announced in the *Intelligencer's* many releases, including the four pictures, cited above. This impressive newspaper page has been photographed and recopied with the Boehm's Church paper's collection.

This rather enormous amount of copy from the *Messenger* reports more, at large, on the devotional and biblical and personal aspects of the gathering. Two long pieces record revealing details.

Testimonies at Boehms

An interesting feature of the Boehm's Chapel Centennial Celebration was the frequent opportunities that were given to those who had been converted at Boehm's or who had been blessed by reason of its existence, to relate their experiences; especially was this so in the oldtime love feast held on Sunday morning, the 20th of September.

The oldest testimony was that quoted from the Rev. William Colbert's journal, that in 1798 he first met the class of Boehm's and "found the greater part of it composed of tender hearted Dutch women."

Amos McAlister said his mother had often spoken of walking from near Lebanon to Boehm's to attend a Quarterly Meeting as early as the year 1810. I was brought to Boehm's by my father and mother 68 years ago. I remember the Church as it was, the high pulpit, the large gallery and also the big wood stove. I was very warm one night, though not from the heat of the stove; the preacher had preached from the text "How shall we escape if we neglect so great salvation." The sermon went to my heart and the fire burned. When the minister talked to a young man by my side, I could scarcely stand it, it was so hot. I hold this place as a very sacred spot. Here my father and mother were wont to come throughout their long lives, thinking it no hardship to walk or ride many miles to get here, but esteeming it a privilege.

Mrs. Martha Morrison, of Hightstown, N.J., who is now in her 93rd year, widow of the late Rev. Robt. Morrison, said: We attended meetings held only in private houses and barns, and when we were permitted to attend a Quarterly Meeting at Boehm's Church, you may be sure it was a great event in our life. This was the first Methodist Church I ever attended, and I rode on horseback, accompanied by my brothers, George and John W. Swift, from Fulton House, our home, a distance of 14 miles. We were hospitably entertained at the Boehm's homestead. I remember distinctly my testimony at that love feast; it was in these words: "I know that Jesus Christ hath power on earth to forgive sins, for he hath forgiven mine." 76 years have passed since then, and I have borne witness to his saving grace. "Christ Jesus is the same yesterday, today and forever."

Brother Jacob Rohrer, of Strasburg, said: Being justified by faith I have peace with God. 63 years ago I put my name on the class roll in this Church, and am so glad to meet in this hallowed place on this centennial occasion. I was an ignorant youth, and when I learned that I must become a new creature I was afraid, and even when I began to see the light I cried out "Not now, Lord." I was afraid I would die while the change was taking place. But I thank God I was born again and am yet alive and propose to live forever with the Lord. When the preacher announced that the people should bring their quarterage the next Sunday, I was ashamed that I did not know what that meant, but I asked the leader of the class and he told me I should bring the one-fourth of what I could afford to give to the Lord to support the Gospel during the year.

I had fifty dollars at home; I took seven dollars of it with a thankful heart to give as my quarterage, but I was much disappointed when the leader told me he would not take it. I thought he meant I must bring more, but I found he would not let me give it all, saying that "I was a poor boy and could not spare so much". I found that he only gave one dollar and he was rich. This hurt me. I thought the Lord could not have been so good to him as he was to me, or he would have given more of his possessions to the service of God. We poor souls were poorly instructed in giving; some of us have not learned it yet. How can I give enough to him who gave his life for me. Here, Lord, I am; take me and all that I have.

Brother Daniel Rinier said: I praise the Lord this love is overflowing this morning. Fifty-three years ago I found Christ. To-day I am happy in the Lord. Many times I have seen these benches filled with souls seeking Jesus. I have also seen this church in its dark hours. In 1857, I was summoned to the bedside of a dying girl at Willow Street, and from my feeble attempts to lead souls into light a revival of religion began.

Bro. S. M. Myers said: We sang awhile ago, "O what a shout when we all get there." I like a shout here, Hallelujah! I love to think of the history of this Church. I am a Methodist out and out. I owe all I am to the Methodist Church. I could not afford to get away. I have been in the Church over 48 years. I like the old style - the altar work, deep conviction, clear conversion, then class meetings are attended with pleasure. I feel at home here in this Church. I expect to shout God's praise in Glory.

Bro. Hackman said: I was brought up to hate the Methodists, but Jesus saved me, and I know it. Glory to God! I love this Methodist Church.

Sermons for A Centennial

The *Messenger's* October issue also ran a characteristically churchly column, submitted by Boehm's pastor C. S. Mervine, in a style of detailed reporting not seen in our time.

The first sermon was preached from John 14:22: "How is it that Thou wilt manifest thyself unto us and not unto the world?" and was by the Rev. Wm. Major of Bethlehem. He was the pastor in charge of Safe Harbor in 1856-57, when the revival occurred at Willow Street under the labors of Bros. Rinier and Brady.

Brother Major related his experience in connection with the reopening of Boehm's Chapel, and stated that it had been his privilege to baptise a large number of people and to receive them into the Class. Bro. Emanuel Stetler was among this number, and his beloved wife, who with many others of the Class have gone home to glory, but a few remain on this side.

Rev. A. J. Amthor was pastor of Boehm's 1992-3. It was during his pastorate that necessary repairs were made in the church....

Bro. Amthor preached from 2 Cor. 4:18: "While we look not at the things which are seen, but at the things which are not seen."

Rev. J. W. Perkinpine, of Port Carbon, pastor of Boehm's in 1888, preached from John 3:16: "God so loved the world."

Rev. C. W. Langley, of New London, junior preacher of Boehm's circuit in 1887, preached from Eze. 28:8-9: "But thou art a man, and no God."

Rev. Wm. Swindells, D. D., of Philadelphia, presiding elder over Boehm's from 1885-9, preached from John 17:22: "The glory which thou gavest me, I have given them."

Rev. W. H. Smith, of Philadelphia, pastor of Boehm's in 1884, preached from Gal. 6:10: "As we have opportunity let us do good."

Rev. F. G. Coxson, of Fernwood, pastor of Boehm's in 1886-7, preached from Gen. 16:23: "Thou God seest me."

Rev. C. F. Turner, of Philadelphia, Presiding Elder over Boehm's from 1873-7, preached from Heb. 4:14: "Seeing then that we have a great High Priest, Jesus."

Rev. J. B. McCullough, D. D., editor of *The Philadelphia Methodist*, junior preacher in charge of Boehm's in 1847, preached from Ps. 17:15: "I shall be satisfied when I awake with thy likeness."

Rev. L. M. Hobbs, of Bossardsville, preached from Acts. 4:13: "They took knowledge of them that they had been with Jesus."

Rev. J. W. Harkins, of Roxborough, pastor of Boehm's during 1879-81, preached from Heb. 6:1, 2, 3: "Leaving the principles of the doctrine of Christ, let us go on to perfection."

Rev. F. M. Collins, of Philadelphia, pastor of Boehm's in 1873, preached from Mark 8:36: "What shall it profit a man if he gain the whole world and lose his own soul?"

Rev. T. B. Neeley, D. D., LL.D., Presiding Elder of Boehm's from 1889-91, gave a historical address based upon I Sam. 7:12, and then preached from Gen. 5:24: "Enoch walked with God and he was not, for God took him."

Rev. J. S. J. McConnell, D. D., of Lancaster, Presiding Elder over Boehm's from 1881-85, preached from Mat. 28:18: "All power is given unto me in heaven and in earth."

Rev. William L. Gray, D. D., Corresponding Secretary of the Tract Society, Presiding Elder over Boehm's from 1867 to 1871, preached from Isaiah 25:6: "A feast of fat things."

Rev. F. M. Brady, of Hammer Hill, pastor of Boehm's in 1876-78, and also fellow-laborer with Daniel Rinier in the revival of 1857, preached from John 8:31: If ye continue in my word, then are ye my disciples, indeed."

Rev. J. G. Wilson, of Avondale, pastor of Boehm's in 1889, preached from John 15:15: "But I have called you friends."

Rev. George Cummins, of Philadelphia, Presiding Elder of Boehm's from 1877 to 1881, preached from Eph. 3:14-17: "For this cause I bow my knees unto the Father of our Lord Jesus Christ."

Rev. Daniel Rinier, local preacher of Conestoga, preached from Prov. 23:23 "Buy the truth and sell it not," or "Get religion and keep it."

Rev. C. S. Mervine, pastor in charge of Boehm's in 1890-91, preached from Acts 5:38: "If this work be of men, it will come to naught."

A *Messenger* Postscript

Reflecting on its centennial day's coverage, the *Messenger* added several informative items.

The thoughtfulness and kindness of Miss Eliza. E. Smith, of Lancaster caused the old arm chair of the Rev. Martin Boehm to be placed in the pulpit of the chapel during the centennial celebration. The table used as a pulpit during the services was also placed there by her kindness. It is the table first used at Millersville by the Methodists as a communion table. Both articles will

probably reach the Conference Historical Society.[35] (Note: The chair has not been presently identified. However, the table is mysteriously present; it is thought to be an existing table which has been in the Chapel chancel over the years. Its substance and features correspond to the period, and it is a treasured item there.)

It was exceedingly kind in Mrs. S. Atmore of Strasburg, to loan for the Centennial the admirable likeness of Bishop Asbury, which was placed on the rear wall of the chapel, just below the likeness of Father Henry Boehm. The picture of the Bishop is not on canvass but on wood, and was painted during one of the good Bishop's sojourns in Strasburg for Mr. Stacy. It is a valued heir-loom in the family.[36]

At the end of these extensive pieces on Boehm's the September *Messenger* wrote this advice: "Preserve this number of the *Methodist Messenger*. Its value will increase as the days go by."

And in October it quipped: **We have heard many pleasant things concerning the September number of the *Methodist Messenger*, as we have with reference to all the numbers that have been issued. We thank our friends for every encouragement.** (Apparently the October "number" was the last issue published! Why?)

CHAPTER 6

QUIET PROSPERITY

Running Account Continues

1893. In 1893 the pastor reported, "...spiritual interest is high: 42 conversions; 46 members received." And in 1896 the Presiding Elder reported "As we move down the river toward the heart of Lancaster County, we skirt the edge of several of the largest circuits within my subdiocese. The first of these is honored by the name of that early pioneer of early Methodism, Father Boehm. A young college-bred preacher was transported from the West to man this circuit. And he has manned it!

"If all circuits were in as good condition as this one, we should wish for more circuits. During the year the modest pastor has witnessed a glorious revival, in which there were fifty conversions and fifty-six probationers. The net increase in membership is forty; churches improved at a cost of $700, and paid on debts $100. The benevolent collections are up. Report has it that a wealthy lady, who is interested in Conestoga, will build a chapel to that church; or, what would be better, a church to that chapel."

1897. The next four years mark advance at Boehm's. The Rev. D. Gollie was pastor 1897-1900. The Presiding Elder's report, now a regular part of Annual Conference reporting, gives a clear, interesting summary of some happenings. "A genuine Pentecostal baptism was experienced by all who gathered in the renovated 'Old Boehm's Chapel' September 13th, the occasion of their 104th anniversary. At the close of the service they willingly gave $300, the last payment on the improvements. Conversions at Boehms."

"Boehm's Circuit has purchased a new $750 parsonage that is easily worth $1200. On this they have paid $100. The interest on the remainder is less than the rent they formerly paid!

Sheds at Boehms

"They have also erected sheds at Boehms costing $200, beside paying off old floating debts of $50. In this undertaking the faithful pastor has been helped by Miss Elizabeth Smith, of Lancaster, who purposes to do still more for Lancaster County Methodism. To her grateful thanks are due."

"Old Boehms Circuit, under the leadership of their indistinguishable pastor, has witnessed a most powerful work of grace. For 22 weeks the services were continued with unabated zeal, the results being the conversion of 226 souls with 186 probationers and 24 members added to the church."

The "Circuit Parsonage" referred to here was at nearby Bumgardner. It was built and later, then sold by the church to Mr. Edward Dagen, who was living there in 1943, one of the older members of the congregation. He related that the house cost him $1100!

The Circuit Is Named Boehm's

1898. The 1898 Minutes record "Boehms" as the circuit's name, for the first time. One wants to ask: why not sooner, this captioned Boehms Circuit, given the acclaimed history there and also the gathering centrality of its ministry, at Boehms?

1899. 1899, at Boehms, "as an after harvest of last year's great revival, 75 souls were garnered...on Boehms Circuit Bro. Gollie has well nigh violated the law of physics and has been in several places at almost the same time. He has held revival services at the three churches; has renovated Marticville Church and paid for it; has secured plans for a new church oat Boehms, which will be built as soon as the weather permits. It will $6,000. $3,000 has been raised. The pastor says they will dedicate without debt. If he says so, this is the way it will be."

Boehms New Church Building, 1899. The cornerstone for the new church was laid June 11, 1899 and the church dedicated November 26th. The District Superintendent's report said of it "The new structure cost $7000. It is one of the most tasteful and convenient country churches we have ever seen..." (Note the significant angle of this photo which catches the tying shed next to the Chapel...built there sometime around 1892. It is not known when the shed was removed.)

A New Church At Boehms

"The cornerstone of the new Boehms Church was laid on June 11, 1899 and the church dedicated by Bishop Walden on November 26th. The old building stands intact, to be used as a chapel.

"The new structure cost $7,000, on which $1,000 yet remains. It is one of the most tasteful and convenient country churches we have ever seen. It will forever be a fitting reminder of the laborous and exceedingly successful work done by the pastor. A great revival has consecrated the building to a continuation of the old-fashioned Methodist work wrought in the past, at this historic spot...sixteen churches report conversions, ranging from fifty to one hundred and twenty-five. They are Boehms...."

1902. The Minutes for 1902 report "fifty-one conversions and 46 accessions. $263. paid on old debts, and $151. on parsonage and improvements. Benevolence collections will advance 50%. Brother Hinkel has endeared himself to the people on the charge and if returned an advanced salary."

1903. "6 conversions; $700. paid on debts and improvements. 1904, 16 conversions."

1905. "The year has been marked by 'Quiet Prosperity'; conversions have occurred in nearly every charge, but...Boehms has been visited with a gracious revival. Also this year the circuit name was changed to 'Boehms and Clearfield'..."

Boehm Becomes A Single Station

1906. Purchased the parsonage, formally belonging to the circuit. "A revival was supplemented by successfully exterminating the $2,200 debt." Conference minutes, now more descriptive of local church work and reports, will pretty much give the words here for the remaining years' history. Also, data will be taken to form a statistics table, showing some annual comparisons. Since pastors' names appear in Appendix A, they will not be repeated here.

The West Willow Story

1907. "At Boehm's a new Sunday School and preaching appointment has been organized, at West Willow. A very suitable lot for church and parsonage has been purchased and over $1200 subscribed. This will insure the preservation of Methodism at a very important part of the present Boehms charge." These word introduce the West Willow Story which was obviously a preoccupation for the next year or two. In the quote above it seems clear that West Willow was a Methodist branch. The high Sunday School attendance report implies a joint program there. The name of the charge for 1908 was "Boehm's and West Willow" but only for one year. The following, brief, oral-history report made in 1943, after conversation with the West Willow official board chairman, seems to sum up the story.

"The mission started with a Sunday School opening in the West Willow school house because the church seemed too far (about one mile) *viz:* mud in winter, heat in summer. They met in the Knights of Golden Eagle Hall at West Willow. All this while, five or more years, the group was a part of the Boehm's Church, with a preaching program developed there by the pastor, in the afternoon.

"The West Willow group began to desire a more regular worship service program, offering to pay a share of the pastor's salary, etc., suggesting a morning and afternoon alternative times. The Boehms group would not consider that change or consent. The group then split and West Willow sought help elsewhere."

"The pastor from the Refton United Brethren Church in Christ came as visiting preacher and pastor. Interest grew for a church building, and in 1907 that work was started. The building was dedicated in 1908, and the church became a part of the Refton Circuit, which it remains today."

1916. By 1916, however, Boehm's interests did move "uptown" for that was the year of the Bumgardner's parsonage sale and the building and move to a new parsonage in the village of Willow Street, "...a much more convenient location, at a cost of about $4000, of which $2250. has been paid." (1991: 2810 Willow Street Pike.)

1922. "A new social hall is nearly completed and will be free from debt. Financial obligations, including parsonage debt of $1800 provided for."

1924. "Five conversions. They have had the old historic church renovated with the expectation that the Conference will be visiting this hallowed spot."

For the remaining years of "quietness" before Boehm's next big public occasion, 1929, let a single phrase bespeak an emphasis for each year. 1925, "This time-honored church is still a vigorous society." 1926, "Sunday

Boehm's Family Members. May 18, 1929 a large crowd of friends and family gathered at the Boehm's cemetery for worship and a memorial at the graveside of Martin Boehm, unveiling a new grave stone, on the occasion of the General Conference of the United Brethren Church meeting at Lancaster. Present from Canada were Major William Boehm and Mrs. Colin Beam Campbell, great-great grandchildren of Martin Boehm.

School attendance increased 50%." 1927, "...planning for visitation evangelistic campaign next year." 1928, "Electric lights, installed in the new church."

A New Martin Boehm Gravemarker - A National Gathering

1929. May 18, 1929 The Lancaster newspaper reported the following: **"Never in the history of Lancaster County church affairs has there been such an impressive spectacle as yesterday afternoon, when a thousand men and women met in a little churchyard to do honor to a man who has been buried there for one hundred and seventeen years.**

The occasion was the unveiling of the monument to the memory of Rev. Martin Boehm whose grave is beside the old Boehms chapel, erected by him on the Boehm farm 1791.

What made it such an inspiring scene was the fact that hundreds were present from 28 states in the Union and Ontario, Canada. The United Brethren Church Conference, now in session in Lancaster, was there in a body, while the members of the Methodist Episcopal Church of Philadelphia came also in great numbers.

It was a united church union of members of two great Protestant churches to honor the memory of a Mennonite preacher who became the father and founder of the Untied Brethren in Christ.

It was an international event inasmuch as a great-great-grandson and a great-great-granddaughter came all the way from Canada to unveil the monument. These are Major William Boehm of Canada, an overseas War veteran, and Mrs. Colin Campbell of Winnepeg, Canada. Major Boehm related in his short address some interesting Boehm's reminiscences that were copied from letters written by the Boehms in Lancaster County to the Boehms in Canada.

He also incidentally referred to a visit to the old graveyard, on the first year of the World War when he was in Lancaster on behalf of the War preparations.

He said Lt. Gov. McClain accompanied him to the grave of his ancestors and that he was much impressed with the site his great-great-grandfather selected for a chapel and graveyard. The program which followed lasted for an hour and a half and was listened to with great interest from beginning to end.

"Rev. W. E. P. Hass, D. D. District Superintendent of the Methodist Episcopal Church, presided. Prayer was offered by Bishop Melvin M. Bell, D. D. Church of The

United Brethren in Christ. Address by Bishop E. G. Richardson, D.D., of the Methodist Episcopal Church; address also by Bishop H. H. Fouts, D. D., Church of The United Brethren in Christ; unveiling by Major Boehm, assisted by Albert M. Brenneman and C. L. Graybill of Lancaster.. With a benediction by Rev. G. W. Babcock, D. D., District Superintendent, Methodist Episcopal Church, and singing in charge of Cornelius Hudson, chorister Philadelphia Conference.

Accompanying photos here help to record this historic gathering, explained by the report above. We assume this, 1929 stone to be the third placed at Martin's grave.

Presumably Martin's first original marker was characteristically plain and simple; and we might be wondering what its words were.

Of the second stone, while we do know its wording, we do not have any knowledge of the work wording or time or the occasion for the placing of this pre-1919 stone. (We wonder where it is, and some of us speculate that it was buried in the woods below the chapel!)

One of the noticeable differences in wording is the reference to the Methodist Church relationship. Apparently there is still no complete agreement as to the analysis and the interpretation of that relationship. (Again, some of us are not worried about it because we are sure that Martin Boehm was a genuine, and thoroughly ecumenical and apostolic Christian!)

Unveiling A New Marker. At his gravesite May 18 1929 four hundred Conference representatives from across the nation gathered to remember and do homage to Father Martin Boehm.

Pre-1929 Stone

Here lie the remains of the Rev'd Martin Boehm
who departed this life (after a short illness)
March 23rd, 1912, in the 87th year of his age
Fifty-five years he freely preached the gospel to
thousands and labored in the vineyard of the Lord
Jesus in Pennsylvania, Maryland, and Virginia
among many denominations of Christians, but
particularly the Mennonites, United Brethren and
Methodists, with the last of whom he lived and
died in fellowship.
He not only gave himself and his services to the
church, but also fed the Lord's prophets and
people by the multitudes.
He was an Israelite indeed in whom was no guile.
His end was peace.

1929 Stone

SACRED TO THE MEMORY OF
REV. MARTIN BOEHM
Born Nov. 30, 1725 Died March 23, 1812
and to his wife
EVE BOEHM
Born Dec. 25, 1734 Died Nov. 26, 1822
For 55 years Martin Boehm labored in the vineyard of
the Lord Jesus Christ and preached the gospel
to the thousands in Penna., Maryland and Virginia,
among many denominations, particularly among
Mennonites, Methodists and United Brethren.
Martin Boehm was for some time a member of the
Methodist Episcopal Church. He was elected a
bishop in the Church of the United Brethren in
Christ, when that denomination was founded in the
year 1800. The United Brethren Church honored him
with the office of bishop until his death.
This saint of God gave himself and his service
unselfishly to the church.
His end was peace.

1930. Once more, let a single phrase bespeak one emphasis cited in his report by the District Superintendent for that year. 1930, "the general condition of the church is excellent...the pastor is invited back." 1931, "The 140th Anniversary is celebrated...a gracious revival." 1932, "141st Anniversary celebrated February 21-28th. Epworth League organized." 1933, "Sunday School and church attendance at a high peak." 1934, Prayer meeting revived with splendid meetings and attendance." 1935, "Six conversions, 5 new members."

1936. "Basement in process of improvement. New heating plant." 1937, "11 conversions. 13 preparatory members. 9 new members." 1938, $500 paid on old debts." 1939, "147th anniversary celebrated with special offering of $247." 1940, "148th Anniversary celebrated in November, with a successful revival." 1941, "All services planned to promote worship and Christian decision." 1942, "W.S.C.S. organized. 150th anniversary of First Methodist Chapel in Lancaster County, November 9-16."

By now, the Annual Conference Minutes provided some statistical information which was arranged as follows in 1943, showing some annual comparisons. Since pastor's names appear on page 133 they will not be repeated here.

Year	Salary	Member-ship	Church School	Avg. Attn.
1906	600	190	150	80
1907	600	245	180	150
1908	600	120	75	50
1909	600	130	75	50
1910	600	155	100	75
1911	700	170	110	75
1912	600	160	105	75
1913	600	173	113	45
1914	600	171	98	45
1915	750	196	107	70
1916	850	185	180	120
1917	950	190	185	135
1918	750	201	185	125
1919	750	195	124	53
1920	1000	199	124	60
1921	1025	192	117	64
1922	1025	166	128	41
1923	1300	162	106	60
1924	1300	160	81	60

1925	1300	160	81	60
1926	1300	194	120	75
1927	1400	198	125	70
1928	1500	189	175	75
1929	1500	152	151	81
1930	1500	153	117	83
1931	1700	137	116	85
1932	1700	153	112	100
1933	1700	173	148	115
1934	1275	164	171	109
1935	1500	164	160	120
1936	1500	146	147	110
1937	1500	162	152	100
1938	1500	169	156	109
1939	1500	177	125	117
1940	1500	185	130	135
1941	1400	184	158	112
1942	1400	148	174	105
1943	1400	168	140	94

Let several phrases from the 1943 writing close this chapter. They reflect the observations and attitudes of a Boehm's student pastor, caught up in rapidly changing scenes, and in continuing changing circumstances at Boehms Methodist Episcopal Church, fifty years ago; changes which have not ceased; and promises moving still toward fulfillment.

"...Today the physical conditions of this historic place have been improved...The 1899 church building is finer than the average country church...The parsonage is commodious and comfortably located at Willow Street..."Quiet Prosperity", the summary statement of the pastor in 1904 to his Annual Conference seems applicable also in these years...Memberships has remained about the same (between 1906 and 1991)...Our church has furnished the city churches with many qualified members and leaders!...The benevolence and missions emphases have grown...This is an average rural, and country village congregation...our's is a strong Mennonite Church community...the community is over-churched...the churches might unite or be federated, for a more vital program of Christian leadership in this community...A glorious past lies behind us...a greater future before...and Boehms Chapel will be a shrine marking it...I appeal for her restoration...someone from our congregation who (perhaps) still remembers when she stood alone on the hill back there, (should) endow her for complete restoration and permanent repair..."[37]

Conclusion. This *History of Boehms Chapel* seeks to bring together, with some interpretation, the background and emergence of a significant religious awakening surrounding the settlement of early, colonial south-eastern Pennsylvania, and the influence of the Wesleyan Movement there as symbolized by the 1791 Boehms Chapel building. The facts, descriptions, and historic records made in this report reflect for many of us words sung at Boehms Chapel during all of its 200 years, "God moves in a mysterious way, His wonders to perform." Its inspiration and blessing will continue with us and with the children's children.

CHAPTER 7

THE RELIC OF YEARS AND HEROES
BOEHMS CHAPEL RESTORATION

If, to use George Taylor's artful words, as this chapter head does here, what he wrote for Father Henry Boehm's birthday about Boehm's Chapel in the 1875 *Reminiscences* would cause readers of this history to read and study Taylor's magnificent historic poem, then this intention would be rewarded!

Restoration Started 1975

The first serious consideration for restoration of the Chapel originated with a group of Lancaster District UMC leaders in mid-1975. That year a self-appointed group of interested individuals got-together to talk about Boehms, compare notes, and make recommendations. They took inspiration and motivation from several inducing factors: the gathering influence of the 1976 national bicentennial; the prevailing references to "roots" in contemporary literature, family relationships and institutions; the consequential effect on some of us exerted by active memberships on the UMCs Conference Commission on Archives and History; and recalling my own involvements as a member of that *ad hoc* group, my thirty-five-years-ago recollections of Boehms Chapel in 1975 would not go away.

Other members of that first group included William Sharp, District Superintendent, Alan Holliday, active lay member of 1st UMC Lancaster and president of Science Press, Ephrata; Russell Clayton, Boehm's paster; James Jolly, history teacher at Millersville U.; Donald Aument, active Conference lay member.

Boehm's Chapel Inside, as it appeared, and was seldom opened, except for an occasional, annual observance, between 1899 when it was replaced as the meeting house, and 1990 when restoration was begun. This 1960 photograph is courtesy Lancaster Intelligencer Journal.

The impetus of this first group, then known as the Boehm's Chapel Committee, evolved into the Boehm's Chapel Society. Prior to June 27, 1982, the formation date of the Boehm's Chapel Society, some of the Committee's accomplishments can be listed.

(1) The development of an awareness of historic Boehm's Chapel, through the church and the community - both the EPC, UMC and the Boehm's UMC. For example, during this span of fifteen years, the Boehm's Church has grown in its awareness of the "precious treasure in our midst." It moved from a time in 1975 when only one member could be enlisted to attend an evaluation meeting, to a time in 1990 when Boehm's Church members are among the leading and most expressive members of the goals of the Society,and when the church there is underwriting a pledge of $20,000 toward the restoration costs! Again, as late as July, 1981, Committee Minutes lament, "The relationship of our work to the Trustees of Boehm's UMC is of concern to the Committee. We wonder if some change or improvement can be made...the pastor will see if a more active relationship can be gained through Trustee membership on the Committee."

Likewise, the Annual Conference on behalf of Boehm's awareness have been productive. Though unable or refusing to solicit funds directly from churches in support of Boehm's, the Annual Conference now has official representative members on its Historical Society, and the Conference has designated Boehm's as an official Historic Site; and it recommended the General Conference action which was approved in 1984, when Boehm's Chapel was named an Official Shrine at The UMC, one of twenty-one in the nation.

(2) Also, in 1976 the popular, illustrated colored "blue folder" describing Boehm's Chapel - Symbol Of The United Methodist Church was written and printed for wide distribution. Alan Holiday printed 18,000 copies for the Committee, without charge. It has gone to a second, large printing.

And, that same year, September 26, 1976, the Committee scheduled a Sunday afternoon meeting for cultivating community and church gatherings for artistic and education events.

(3) A second successful printing undertaking by the Committee in 1976, *Martin Boehm* was a monograph life of our venerated Father Boehm, the first to appear in booklet form. Now in its second printing (January 1981), it was

also a contribution of the Boehm's Chapel project from Alan Holliday and Science Press. Our *Martin Boehm* publication has taken its place (at the suggestion of the UMC, GCA&H) along side of the popular biographical series produced and distributed by the UMC, General Commission on Archives and History.

(4) The third printing feat of the Committee, the January 1982 reprinting of Henry Boehm's *Reminiscences* has been, by any comparison, the most significant accomplishment of the Committee. This great, rare old book (the 1875 edition) was reproduced in a beautiful facsimile. Its value increased greatly by the addition of a complete *Index*, also printed by Science Press. It was offered and distributed at the (ridiculously) low price of $12.50. At its publication the Methodist Publishing House agreed to help market the book and give it some publicity. That assistance has not been effective. The *Reminiscences* is still available, its sales still intended to help finance the Restoration.

(5) Another education venture was produced, using also first the popular phrase "Temple Of Limestone" to name a sound filmstrip, which is about the Boehm's history and Chapel background. The audio-visual presentation, produced in color, with the help of local artists and the Eckert Studio at Leola, brings education to schools and churches. A leaflet describing its usefulness was widely distributed. See the adaptations of its script and illustrations in the Introduction Chapter.

(6) Keeping the objective of Preservation and Restoration of the Boehm's Chapel before the church and community was a decided goal of the Committee from the outset. At one of the earliest meetings bringing together the concerns of the Committee and the EPC Historical Society, June 22, 1976, then chair Donald Aument reported to the Society and outlined some of the work underway by the Committee "...sandblast-cleaning the outside walls...replacing window sills...etc...but we talked about the restoration as the main goal...restoring the present ceiling as it was in 1791...replacing the balcony on three sides as it was originally...restoring the high pulpit arrangement...a new split shingle roof...sconces and candle lighting..."

Again, June 27, 1982, at the organizing meeting of the Chapel Society, chair Alan Holliday reviewing work of the Committee, "...stated that six years ago a preliminary architectural study was completed and indications are that (we know enough about the old chapel to proceed with the goal of restoration)...that our prayers and gifts would be in support of this goal and purpose...." The study referred to here was made by the John DeVitry architectural firm of Lancaster. "They offered a projection of an architectural and historical investigation of the Chapel. They referred to their earlier work in 1976 at the Chapel, and submitted a three-page report (prepared by John Snyder) outlining a proposal for completing such a study and preparing its documentation."

Boehms Chapel A Continuing Resource Of Blessing

There have always been some voices raised (some in doubt, some in protest) of restoration. These interested individuals have two objections: first, that the money and the resources required for the restoration should be invested in on-going work and ministry of today's Church, rather than put into restoring an old structure; and that the present building if preserved would stand as a sufficient reminder of the past. "You don't have to restore it to appreciate it."

A second prevailing objection to the restoration activity contends that the future continuing use of the restored building and its facility is, at once, ill-defined and non-essential, in relation to the Call Of The Gospel. "You have not said enough about why you need it."

These two appropriate criticisms are still heard, and they are very much before the Restoration Project planners. Indeed, in every circumstance, "Sacrificial Giving Deserves Not To Be Wasted!"

Fund-raising to meet the restoration goals has received very spotty and sometimes disconcerting attention during this same formative period. The accumulated Minutes and record of meetings both show frequent reference to the subject; as they reflect the committee's struggling both to define and to implement a plan. Estimating the possible costs, casual, early, speculative estimates ranged from upwards of $15,000. to $175,000.

One of the earliest proposals envisaged a cash cost of $15,000., combined with a large regular organized force of volunteers, skilled workers and labor contributions, someone said, "...like unto the Habitat For Humanity experience." (If I may be indulged a personal observation, as a sometimes HFH worker, this proposal, though never seriously considered, might very well have proved to be a very great blessing to the project; and it should be added, in conversation about it, our supervising contractor, Jack Heckles, favored the idea!)

Investigations into a typical, professional fund-rasing campaign were more or less thoroughly explored, in two ways. The UMC has a national program for assistance to Conference and Institutional fund-raising campaigns. Its coordinator and director met in consultation with the Society's Committee. Likewise, the (nationally well-known) Kirby Smith Associates (based in Lancaster Co.) professionals were hired in a study procedure, with the Committee. Both consultations proceeded along very similar lines and with very similar observations about our situation. The Committee was not able, however, to recommend that we undertake the requirements and the expectations of a professional fund-raising campaign.

In contrast, let it be labeled "unstructured fund-raising" ensued. This included a combination of items and strategies such as the following: 1. Continuing membership solicitation, along parameters set around 1982. 2. The scheduling of information and education gatherings, events, and activities, either single ones or in series; some with fund-raising goals, some as a time for receiving cash contributions or collections. These activities, also seemed to enlist the awareness and support of Boehm's UMC constituents in new ways.

3. Emphasis upon program developments and attendance at the time of "Annual Meeting" of the Boehm's Chapel Society. One result of this emphasis had been that Boehm's Chapel has gained the attention and participation of more "Boehm's Family Members." And these members have been able to hold a mini-family reunion at Annual Meeting time! Some Boehms' descendants have become quite active, effective supporters. 4. The manufacture and sale of a variety of created souvenirs, mostly with some attraction to the chapel. A recent, printed brochure lists such "mementos" suggesting contributions from $30. to $500., with these words: "...donations for these mementos made from parts of the building will move us closer...to complete the task...." 5. An information and education project taken to Lancaster District UM Churches. This item requires a brief description.

The United Methodist Church has not been able, at this time, to make an organized response from Conference or General Administration funding in support of the Boehm's

Chapel Restoration Budget. Nor were we permitted to solicit churches or members within these jurisdictions for such a consideration. Both of these decisions could readily be anticipated, and were not exceptional. Also, the present fall back of UMC general church budgeting would have some bearing upon it.

Consequently, concerted effort was made among the seventy-four local, Lancaster District UM Churches, in the continuing interest of Boehms Chapel. The idea was clearly conceived by a group of "local church historians" in a workshop gathering in 1989 that we should try to come up with a plan to reach every member (25,000) of the Lancaster District UM Churches (74) *vis-a-vis* Boehms Chapel.

An *ad hoc* committee developed a program designed to put forward "information and education" about Boehms-Chapel-And-Its-Restoration for 1991. A corps of eighteen "visitors" were enlisted, each to assume responsibility for contacting (@ 4 or 5) churches, with suggestions and a request that the church put-in-place an appropriate program which would commend information and education among their members and their church groups, resulting hopefully in the church collecting a "significant contribution" for the BC Restoration Fund.

At this writing-time, that very "I & E" project, delayed or misguided with some of the churches, is, in fact, still in operation. And, as with the other five "unstructured fund-raising modes" we can anticipate, at some later time, receiving from all of them an itemized,complete report of the various amounts received.

Restoration Accomplished

Time, along with some significant programs and activities (as cited above) combined to produce a resulting, growing awareness of Boehms Chapel. It seemed to be noticeable with churches (including the Boehm's Church); community levels of interest; and with more and more individuals. With all of these concerned, the target date - *Birthday-Time, 1991* - seemed like just around the corner. There were a few scattered voices raised to concede a later finishing-date, but fortunately both laity and clergy members of these groups kept urging the necessity for restoration to be accomplished by party-time, mid-June 1991. That apparently is still a strong driving factor. The Caldwell, Heckles & Egan, general contractors, chosen because of their reputation and experience in restoration projects, are continuing to fashion the parts and put them back together. Their rep, Jack Heckles, has maintained a super relationship with the project and with our coordinators and workers.

Concurrent with this growing interest and concern, three major perceptions emerged. 1) We, are eager and willing to proceed, but we must pay-as-we-go. 2) We need, if possible, to find a (local) coordinator/manager who will work with the general contractor in the restoration work. 3) One possible solution to the lack of cash on hand would be to take the work in "phases" - time-line and accomplishment-and-pay phases.

The three objectives named above are, indeed, working guidelines, as Restoration is moving ahead. There is no record of a loan or borrowing cash. The second need, finding a general manager was accomplished when Earl Cramer, a superior craftsman now retired executive director, the Lancaster County Home Builders Association, agreed to work in this assignment. Earl's untimely death, just as he was getting started with Restoration, brought sorrow to many of us and a transition to the project. Fortunately, another Boehm's member and Trustee, David Hess, from quite a different background and experience, was inspired to take on the leadership job. David has given immeasurable time and tireless attention and appreciable skill to this leadership position; deserving of the greatest appreciation.

The "phase" idea, as the work progressed and now moves to completion, seems less relevant. However, it did guide the work's beginning; and it also furnishes a framework for a brief description here, in telling of some major changes and reconstruction; though I'm sure this resume will perhaps not catch all of some important points in the report.

To note that the "phases" have now been put out of the original sequence, is also to see how a lot of skill and hard work in management and workmanship on the part of workers and the contractor have resulted in significant savings but at the same doing excellent work. This is an unbeatable combination, and its report needs to be retold. In June, 1987 contractual cost estimates put the total at over $175,000. Four years later, increasing costs trends notwithstanding, the workers and planners have reduced the total to less than $150,000.

Phase I saw the roof structures and ceiling completely

rebuilt, the original, high ceiling replaced, and outside a new shingle roof maybe the first, again since its original. And the unique, old "pent roof" was back over the entrance steps and doorway. This work was done by June's Annual Meeting 1990.

Phase II included a total new floor system; excavating a crawl space and pouring a concrete base under the floor; new retaining walls under the stone foundation areas. At this time also provision was being made for a total new electrical service to the building, and it serves to illustrate the times when hand labor and machine rentals without charge were real cost-cutting, plus a proudly reported gift from PP&L in the electrical wiring costs. Observe also here that the space under the floor was to house a ventilation system. Rather, instead a gas furnace was found to be a better facility, and space was developed under the raised-end of the balcony for its installation.

References to floor-structures and excavating require some mention her of a dispute in the procedures, with reference to the minority-opinion proposal that the basement space should be excavated, in a "now-or-never" situation. The recommendation, rejected by vote in a Chapel Society meeting, was based on the concurring consideration of its feasibility by the supervising contractor, and the "tentative" agreement of a possible donor gift for the required, additional cost. The ostensible rationale for the negative vote was the opinion that to excavate would too radically change the original forms and dimensions of the chapel. Some of the words that were written in an appeal letter to that prospective donor might serve to record the positive benefits envisaged in the excavation proposal.

It said, "...but in addition to restoring the ancient building to its original forms, there are two related projects that should receive some attention at this time. One, some thought should be given to the addition of a museum site at Boehms. Two, the basement area of the old building should be opened, as a permanent plus to the continuing use of the building. And the striking part of these two considerations is the way in which they are related!

"...At present there is no designated Wesleyan-Methodist Archives and History Center in this area. But there should be such a Center because this is one of our nation's most historic regions, and therefore it is probably just a matter of time until there will be such a "center" in the Lancaster District. Such a center would enhance our education and evangelism ministries.

"Structurally and strategically, now is the time to excavate that basement area. The contractor says it is possible. It is proposed that we try to see developed there a significant resource center, at the basement area of old Boehms Chapel..."

(As a proponent of the basement-excavation proposal, based on the positive features expressed in the correspondence above, I can say this is my personal, greatest disappointment with the Restoration. I also feel it is only a matter of time (5 years; 10 years; 30 years?) until a time when, again we will wish we had, indeed, excavated the basement; and thus put into good use the extra space under the same roof.)

Phase III called for removal of the 1883 doors and large windows, and the installation of the replacement balconies on three sides. Here, too, the actual timing has changed, although new restored paneled galleries are now in place. We should note the artful, skilled masonry work achieved inclosing the stone "holes" above the windows. *"You can't hardly see 'em"* does express the good job there! There is some lament about the (beautiful, period) brick arches which once appeared above the windows, according to all indications, from the beginning (*viz*: the earliest, only photograph of the Chapel; and the convincing presence and authority of the cope-shoulders in the stone-work on both sides of the original window top's location, more pronounced on some windows than on others.

Phase IV outlined one of the more visible parts, the renowned, classic "high pulpit" also a lot of essentials: the installation of new interior walls, plaster ceiling and walls; insulation all around; wood finishes; interior wiring, etc. One of the most baffling yet, obviously, thoroughly fascinating items is the "high pulpit." It attracts more attention and finds more references by those who wrote or talked and "remember" the old chapel. Its exact elevation and its exact appearance may not be fully duplicated. The reference by 1891 celebrators who talked about its height and especially in relation to the window there, that standing on the platform the high window could be adjusted, is of special interest. The "reconstruction crew" feel they can come up with a good match of what it looked like in 1791! At the time of this writing the high pulpit is one of the last (most intriguing) items to be put in place, before mid-June. I hope our proposal for a

Boehms Chapel Restored, 1991. This most recent photo of the Chapel shows some of its new features, the inside Restoration changes, the work completed in time for Restoration Ceremonies held June 22-23, 1991 - notably the restored heightened ceiling; the replaced paneled gallery on three sides; the consequent shortened, new windows; the new pews; and the new "high pulpit." (You will please place here the photograph you take of it. We missed the deadline!)

last-minute illustration to include the new pulpit will be allowed. Otherwise, you sketch in the picture on that page here left for it!

True, once restoration is completed, then legitimate uses of the restored building are clearly required of us - in continuing Christian education, and mission, and evangelism. In every association, we will be trying to anticipate the requirements and the continuing needs for creative uses of the (new) Chapel.

We are praying that it might, indeed, be a significant resource and learning center for those sojourners who pass by here - both the "saved" and the "unsaved" (to employ two very popular and meaningful words from 1791) and those who are seeking to "grow in God's grace" inspired by Wesleyan-styled ministries in the Church - as they continue their Christian pilgrimage into the 1990s and on into the tricentenary.

Counting on our faithfulness in the ministry of the Gospel, surely Father Martin Boehm would approve what we are doing here!

SOME LAST WORDS

Meet My Father - by Henry Boehm

The following is a pretend address by his son (edited for this publication) delivered by the author at the annual meting of the Strawbridge Shrine Association. This historic statement combines both factual information and interpretative opinions, expressive of the Boehm's legacy to the Church. Let it be an historic epilogue.

It's spring-plowing time - Conestoga, Lancaster County, Pennsylvania - in that side field, to the west from the barn. They had just finished clearing it through to the back side, out to the road that runs south towards our church at Byerland. My father had been plowing there most of the day. Plowing was legitimate; he'd learned and he liked it, to work hard all the day long - but he was really preoccupied - for still additional weeks and months, as his spiritual agonizing continued.

He had been called to preach. But in his teaching and his preaching he knew only frustration and uncertainty. Until this one day in spring of 1759, while plowing there in the field and struggling in prayer (down on his knees, with the plow handles as a "bench") he said (later) an experience of blessing, and peace, and power, in the Holy Spirit seemed to be poured into his soul!

And you'll forgive me if I say it again, in this context today: except for that experience of father's at the plow, I would not be here with you as I am today reporting; my family would not be all that it was so wonderfully; my father would not have been so led out in the ministry. Except for that day in the field, the United Brethren in Christ Church - that great indigenous branch in the early settlements of our great Methodist Church - would probably not be. Except for that day in the field, the day Robert Strawbridge first came to our house in Conestoga, in the Pequea Settlement, in Lancaster County, would probably not have its day in history. Except for my father's experience, and my mother's affirmation of it, we would not have know what on earth Strawbridge was talking about!

I'm glad that you asked Abe Sangrey to come here today.

And I'm glad that he got Ed Schell's permission to bring me along. For Abe and for me it's much more than just nice friendly feelings, to be here. Once more the Lord is in this place. Praise His Name!

I see two big things that need to be done here: One, to make sure we know my father, Martin Boehm; the other, that we try to identify him placed clearly among our founders, as if to answer the question, if possible: Martin Boehm, "so what"?

Just by way of clarity, that two-fold aim is quite like what I understand the Christian preacher's goal is in proclaiming the Gospel: the teacher/preacher of the Good News wants to make sure, first, that he and everybody else do their best to get the biblical material on the right trail; and second, to be able to see and to hear what the message is for us today. Such biblical searching is called *exegesis* - (or exposition) a critical examination or explanation of the text. And the second step is called *homiletical interpretation* - an attempt to identify and to update the report; as if to answer the question, "so what"?

The exegesis is: The Martin Boehm of History. The homily is: a series of questions such as: what do we do and where do we go with Martin Boehm? Was he saint or otherwise? Is he for us or against us? And one exciting question might be to ask: "If Martin Boehm were alive and well in the Church in 1991, where would he be and what would he be doing?" Again, "What should be our attitude today about his expulsion, two hundred years later?" How do *you* explain Martin Boehm.

Apologies, if I spend too much time, in the first place then, with the Martin Boehm of history. But that's in your blood. It's certainly in mine! We need to keep retelling the story. Let's not get tired of repeating the story. Perhaps more than we can know, as Muriel Rukeyser has said, "The universe is made of stories, not of atoms." And as Abe's daughter has put it, writing in a piece she had published, "Listen to the stories. The power is in the stories!" So, the story of Martin Boehm....

His father, Jacob the III was on that famous ship, Maria Hope, in 1715, to arrive with that second group of Mennonites coming to Herrville, Pequea, Conestoga. And just over the hill to the west from soon-to-be-famous "Herr House", a 381 acre plot was subdivided for my grandfather Jacob Boehm. And here with his bride Barbara Kendig, they began to clear a patch of land and to share in the honor of breaking ground for one of the very first farms in Lancaster County. And here on Nov. 30, 1725, a son, Martin Boehm, my father was born.

Born among Mennonites - Mennonites in Europe for at least tow generations. His great-grandfather, Jacob I, a member of the Swiss-Reformed Church; his grandfather, Jacob II, the first Mennonite among them. It was he who "came over". Maybe he was the first maverick among them! If perchance all of this "kicking over the traces" started with Jacob II, we would then stop for just a minute with him.

I tell of it here, early, in my book, *Reminiscences* (which the Boehm's Church people have so exquisitely reprinted). It was one of our famous family stories - told and retold. Leaving the Swiss farm he had become a tradesman, apprentice, as a young journeyman he traveled the country.

In his wanderings Jacob fell in with a people called Pietists...he was converted among them. The change was so great when he returned home, his language so strange that his friends could not understand him...this singular experience; his criticism of formal religion; his boldness in reproving sin - raised a storm of persecution. The home folks pastor renounced him as a heretic. His father reprimanded him. Grandfather was convicted of heresy and sentenced to prison.

An older brother was appointed to conduct him to the prisonhouse. He did not watch his brother closely, and as they traveled near the border of Switzerland and France, grandfather escaped (over into the Palatinate). Now he was free from domestic and priestly persecution.

There it was that young Jacob became acquainted with a people called Mennonites. He united with them and soon became a lay elder. Married into a Mennonite family, one of his son's, Jacob III, my grandfather, was born 1693. He emigrated to this country in 1715.

My grandfather was induced to come to America from the glowing description given of this country by Martin Kendig, one of the seven families who had settled in what is now Lancaster County, PA. (p. 9-11)

That's part of what I wrote about my family in 1865. I would probably have said more in detail, if I could have realized how eager you would be these days, to know and to have more of the details. For one, I would have said "uncle Martin Kendig". Perchance, "Miss Kendig" was

Martin's sister, rather then sister-in-law of Christian Herr (of Hans Herr fame).

Sadly, you feel, so little is known about my father's early life, and you know even less about grandfather's home and Barbara Kendig Boehm, his mother. His education was through his home and his church. The language of both was German. There was a school house and the teacher "boarded from house to house." Father did learn English also, and he had a library (which was significant enough and his library gets singular mention in his will!). For serious study in English it included Wesley's *Sermons* and John Fletcher's *Checks* (another Wesleyan movement commentary).

What little bit you do have written seems so precious if not priceless! Two sketches from my book do give a glimpse into our home, and also the hearts, I think, of Martin and Eve Boehm. At age ninety, of Eve, my mother, I wrote:

My early advantages for religious instruction were great. I was brought up in the nurture and admonition of the Lord. Morning and evening the old family Bible was read and prayer was offered. My father's voice still echoes in my ears. My mother too had much to do in molding my character and shaping my destiny. One evening as I returned home I heard a familiar voice engaged in prayer. It was my mother (praying). Among other things she prayed for her children, and mentioned Henry, her youngest son....

And this is how I remembered my father's influence:

When I was about fifteen I went to learn the milling business, and worked in a grist mill. There I had no religious counsel or example. What a critical period it is when a young man leaves home. I went into bad company, supposing my father would not hear of it; but I was mistaken. He did hear of my conduct, and he came to see me. When I saw him I suspected his errand. A guilty conscience needs no accuser. The plain, solemn, affecting reproof he gave me at that time had a wonderful effect upon me. His quivering lip (as he talked with me), his tearful eye, and his tremulous voice showed how deeply he felt for me." (p. 16)

Apparently you take pride in your 1991 conclusion that people felt good about Martin Boehm - in his family, in his church, the local congregation and out in the community - that Martin Boehm was a good man; that he was a man of God. I agree, from the best standards we know, his name could have been Nathan!

There are many ways that Mennonite Christians express such mutual care and support for each other. But perhaps there is no greater evidence of strong community feeling than when Mennonites select a minister. In his case the inspiring choice by lot. It was 1756; father was 31.

The nomination from his friends and family at Byerland Church had come in the first place because "for the past two years he had been giving testimony at the close of the sermons, and frequently concluded the meeting." But the crunch came the next Sunday - following his successful sharing in the lot - he had been requested to preach. He had memorized scripture. He thought he was prepared. He had prayed "to the Lord to assist me in retaining the Word, and to strengthen me in my weakness." But in this first attempt to preach, he could only "stammer out a few words, and then be obliged to sit down in shame and remorse."

As I said in opening, his day in the field changed all of that! And we just cannot talk about father's leadership in the Church, or his gifts in the ministry, without first citing and understanding his very personal, spiritual, struggle and the subsequent awakening of his personal conversion experience.

Now, for the first time in two years his soul was at peace. Now he "wished next Sunday were tomorrow morning", he said. Sunday came, and Martin preached with new power and new freedom. In the weeks that followed, "it was the same and much more." "Now" he said "the Scripture, before mysterious and like a dead letter to me, was plain."

It has always interested me to note that this religious awakening came to father, at a time, after his call to the ministry. Two years later it was, after his bishop, Jacob Hostetter, had died in 1761, father was advanced, again by lot, to the position of Bishop. Surely this second affirmation served also to reinforce the powerful sense of personal liberation and blessing which had come in his religious experience. At this same time also he was led out into paths of ministry and service abroad. As members of the Mennonite Society, including his own family, had begun to migrate westward and south to Maryland and Virginia, his influence and his circuit riding went with them.

And perhaps, more important for you here, these were the very years when the first circuit riders for the

English speaking Wesleyan movement were being welcomed by his father Jacob into his home, in Conestoga. I know it's of real interest to you, all; and I'm sorry I didn't try to write more about those first visits to our County. I could have set it all straight for you; but it's too late now. The one time that I did write about Robert Strawbridge visiting our place, I was six years old, in 1781. (Abe Sangrey thinks that Strawbridge and other Wesleyan circuit riders were in Boehm's country much earlier; maybe in the 1760s.) You do remember, (I had written) the first Class was organized at our house in 1775, and very early on my mother was a member!

You may never know for sure that the beloved George Whitefield ever came to Boehms, but his influence was unmistakable. And just as surely, at this time, God's man, Martin Boehm, was being raised up, on behalf of the Gospel, among the "Dutch" in that very same "endless line of splendor".

Abe Sangrey says it all began in the 1760s - this "riding for the Gospel" among the "Dutch", parallelled by the English circuit riders in the colonies. And "Conestoga Crossroads" was becoming a pivotal point here, as Martin Boehm's legacy to history was being formed, as he pioneered among the Mennonites in the colonies, opening the way - if not indeed fashioning the future - for later itinerant ministries among the German speaking followers of Christ.

While doing the Gospel in this new way, Martin Boehm was discovering others who were having experiences very similar to his own, independent experience. (Recall, just in passing, that the renowned meeting with Philip Otterbein at Long's Barn was May 1767.)

Throughout the colonies, circuit riding ministries were seen to provide a vehicle for the emphasis in *Pietism.* Pietism how it made provision for: (1) Bible Reading; (2) Personal Testimony and Witnessing; (3) Personal Confession and Lay Counseling in the Brotherhood; (4) Hymn Singing; (5) Free Prayer; (6) Kneeling to Pray; (7) Shared Testimony of Personal Religious Experience; (8) Meetings At Times Other Than Sunday, including the evening; and in (9) Other Places Than The Church; "Great Meetings" a forerunner of the Campmeeting! If you, too are making comparisons - or looking for 1991 facsimiles of the Church in your time - just look again at these nine discoveries which my father and Bishop Francis Asbury had made 200 years ago!

These new forms for expressing the faith carried Martin Boehm beyond the confines of his own congregation. His fame - a term he would have rejected! - was confirmed by his good pastoral relations at home and by his ability in itinerant preaching away from home. Martin Boehm was a leader, if not the first, among the Pennsylvania Dutch to participate in this outreach and development. He seemed to enjoy responsibility.

The Mennonite Church had raised up a son; early-born of persecution; nurtured in the "good news" among a group of families who must be considered a singular colony of heaven; among a people who were also called to write for posterity a new chapter in the never-ending record of the *Book Of Acts* - The Book Of Acts In The Pequea Settlement! Such a son - as if for such a time as this, he was raised up!

We have always said that new power in the Holy Spirit and new freedom emerged for Protestants in Europe. These new styles came to the Mennonites through *Pietism* and *Anabaptism* traditions. And one of the baffling contradictions is that two short generations later, Mennonites themselves, now, in the colonies were not able to accept, in freedom, in some cases, the protests and upward-bounding of the Spirit which seemed clearly to come to many of the Mennonite Christians.

Martin Boehm was upward-bounding! As you know, the penalty for this "enthusiasm" about the Gospel and his evangelistic style was excommunication. After all attempts at reconciliation had failed, it was about 1775 that my father was put out of the Mennonite Church.

1775 is a pivotal year around Boehms. It's the year a recorded Methodist Class was organized at our house.

In that singular book, written a hundred years later, titled: *The Mennonite Church And Her Assusers*, Martin Boehm is first on the list. Apparently father felt, as did John Wesley, that it was not his job to be popular, but rather to be prophetic!

There is every indication that Martin Boehm neither planned nor desired to leave the Mennonite Brotherhood. In his heart be probably never separated. He never ceased to wear his plain clothes. He also did not cease his labors in the ministry.

For the remaining 37 years of his life he served local and area congregations; traveled widely; assisted and encouraged the movement and the organization of the United Brethren in Christ Church (which group, also, named father their Bishop, there in 1800); all, in a word, history has recorded and labeled him a major figure in the revival movement in colonial and new-nation Protestantism.

Reflecting on his dismissal, when once later interviewed by a church historian of his day, what Martin said summarizes his attitude and his work: **My labors were owned of the Lord in the awakening and conversion of souls. Many were brought to a knowledge of the truth. But it was a strange work; and some of the Mennonite meetinghouses were closed to me. Nevertheless I was received in other places....I now preached the Gospel spiritually and powerfully....I was excommunicated from the Mennonite Church on a charge truly enough advanced: of holding fellowship with other societies and preaching in different languages.** (from Spayth, *History Of The United Brethren Church*)

Not all Mennonites were expelling the revivalists. Martin's success in the ministry attests not so much to Mennonites' change to revival systems, but also to the influence Mennonites had upon the revival movement. Hear Mennonite researcher Sem Sutter comment: "It is wrong to assume...that all Mennonites who viewed the revival movement with sympathy left the church, and that all Mennonites who remained in the church opposed revivals. In the organized group that finally came together with Martin Boehms as leader, to establish the United Brethren in Christ Church, in 1800, nearly one-half of its ministers were former Mennonites!

So, the Martin Boehm story - the report of the historic person - the saga of events - the exegesis - is perhaps quite enough for many of us....That it's enough just to hear a retelling of the story....That we can be trusted to fill in behind the story for our own edification and guidance in 1991.

Once when my friend Abe Sangrey had told our Bishop James Ault about it, when first he read the full story of Martin Boehm, Ault replied, "In an era when immorality in every personal and social form threatens the very fabric of our society, to recall the life of a good man (Martin Boehm) whose purpose was to share with joy the good life, is in itself a good thing to do." And this, then brings us to the interpretation.

It is true, that mostly in our generation, the researchers do not put Martin Boehm down. Generally my father gets fairly high grades in your generation! Sangrey was saying there is a way we can talk about how the Martin Boehm story illuminates your own situation...how Martin Boehm might be seen to influence your Church and your Society...as Faith-Father to some...as Spiritual-Director to many.

Abe Sangrey tends to be too apologetic. But he makes no apology for his enthusiasm and his affirmation about our need to learn from the Martin Boehm story. To illustrate, he says there are a couple of radical ideas which do need to be put forward...and that very abbreviated. He has one suggestion for the Mennonites; one for Methodist Historians; and a third for the United Methodist Church Council Of Bishops...three samples, to help make the point.

First, note that the time when the Mennonites put father out of their Church, there was so much double-talk; so much misunderstanding; so much disunity about it, in the Conference and around his home church at Byerland. Now that the light of 200 years has passed, let's ask the Mennonites to do something about that. It might be too radical, but let's note that there is some precedent for it (we'll go into that next time). Here's a chance to set things straight with Father Boehm. Is it too much to ask, or to assume, that the Lancaster Mennonite Conference should take official action to rescind their earlier decision in that expulsion? Could the Mennonites say officially, "Martin Boehm, we apologize."

Second, Methodist historians, all: you have yet to realize and to report it, a major result of your merging conference, viz-a-viz Lancaster County, Pennsylvania, when in 1968 you merged and named it the United Methodist Church. To be sure, never prior to 1968. But when you brought those three historic bodies together, the geography of their beginnings took on the most singular change. The greatest number of the original *people* and the original *places*, and the original *events*, which you identify with the United Methodist Church, are in and adjacent to Lancaster County, Pennsylvania - more perhaps that anywhere else in the country! "Conestoga Crossroads" is perhaps the most pivotal point of all places! And the United Methodist Church has not yet in its history-reporting and in its story-telling, either paid enough attention to it, nor reported it fully - the Mennonite side of its history....

The facts surrounding this assertion cry out for attention. Our historians talk at length about where it was that Methodism came to the new nation. Wonderful reports are made from Robert Strawbridge and Maryland's Sam Creek area about mid-1760s. And from Philip Embury, up there in New York area about mid-1760s. But have you considered the interesting possibility, now that you are, indeed, the United Methodist Church, that when the story from Boehm's Country in Pennsylvania is fully told you just might not have to continue that debate. Your Father-In-God, Bishop Martin Boehm, was ordained into the apostolic, Christian ministry in Pennsylvania in 1756!

The *third* suggestion and request is made to our Council Of Bishops. You can be sure my father would never want to talk about this. But let us be clear. It's more than a gag.

It is true, Francis Asbury and Thomas Coke were consecrated in 1784. The listing, then, of our bishops, (as in the front of the Discipline) next puts the name of Martin Boehm and William Otterbein third and fourth, dated 1800. But Martin Boehm was selected to be a bishop in 1761 "on behalf of the Apostles" a selection the Methodist Church recognizes. Martin Boehm functioned as a bishop 25 years before Father Asbury even dared to fulfill Jesus' command (in Matt. 28:19). If we are serious about the emerging history report of our great Church, maybe this is the year. It's an interesting idea: perhaps Martin Boehm was the first bishop of the United Methodist Church! And, for sure someday, the Council Of Bishops will take action to change the listing. My father deserves, so to be remembered!

Abe wanted me also to tell how he's been helped by some guidelines suggested by author Carl Gustafson in his outline of *The Significance Of History*. He says, in the *first place*, look, it can be seen as *entertainment*.

If that means, as indeed it does, engagement or interest holding, then perhaps it's okay to want to be entertained by the Boehm's story. Principal historian of the Evangelical Association, Raymond Albright, has said of the arrival of grandpap's ship the Maria Hope, in 1710, at Philadelphia: it should be likened in its significance unto the coming in 1620 of the Mayflower, in New England! And he goes on to say that the work of Martin Boehm, Philip Otterbein, and Jacob Albright, around the close of the 18th century can be likened unto the Great Reformation, three centuries later. So, entertainment! Wow!

Our analyst also says of history, *secondly*, it's an

opportunity and a *call to memorialize our ancestors*. I believe everyone of us (and I urge it) should have at least one person whom we take on as our model, the one we're going to imitate. Someone, that is, whom we can say, I'm committed to do the research to try to know more about that person than anyone else knows about him/her. And allow, by God's grace, she become my inspiration. Maybe a member of your very family (Now hear this, ye genealogists) or the most famous person in your history. Among them, such a person, for some people I know is Martin Boehm. Memorializing our ancestors. Wow!

Thirdly, Gustafson says the significance of history is for *inspiration and warning*. One of our most blessed Christian ideas in the Church is that we desperately need one another in the human experience. And let us indeed count our blessings - how in your history and in mine, in Pietism and in Wesleyanism, we are required to do so. Indeed, let us celebrate: ideas we've introduced: "society", "conference", "love", "one another"! Now when you take that standard and elevate it into Christian theology, it means that God has things to say to me through others, which if I don't hear, I will never hear! Bishop Asbury was right, when at my father's funeral in 1812 he exhorted:

O rising generations, who have so often heard the prayers of this man of God in the houses of your fathers. O, ye Germans, to whom he has long preached the word of truth. Martin Boehm, being dead, yet speaketh. O, hear his voice from the grave - exhorting you to repent, to believe, to obey.

I do need to hear that. For inspiration and for warning. Praise The Lord.

And *fourthly*, he suggests, for history as a tool, it helps us contemplate *how we got to where we are*. The major source, about the Boehm's story, is the *Reminiscences*. This 1865/1875 classic, antique book - a beautiful reprint. One of the priceless parts of is an historic, epic poem (8 pages, 203 lines) Greek-Ode style poem, about this time and location and its place in history. It was written and red and dedicated at my 100th birthday party. Three lines go as follows:

Where are our hero fathers; the prophets, do they live forever? Honor, all honor today, to the men and their triumphs. Labors that shaped a new world, and triumphs that echo through heaven.

Praise The Lord!

APPENDIX A

Circuit Riders and Ministers who have served Boehms United Methodist Church

At Boehm's Home

1775	Richard Webster
1776	Samuel Spragg
1777	Robert Lindsay
1778	
1779	Joseph Cromwell
1780	John Cooper, George Mair
1781	Wm. Gelndenning, Samuel Row, Isaac Rollins
1782	William Partridge
1783	Reuben Ellis, John Haggerty, Thomas Haskins
1784	LeRoy Cole, Joseph Cromwell, Jeremiah Lambert
1785	Thomas Vasery, Ira Ellis, James Thomas
1786	Caleb Boyer, Henry Ogbourn, Peter Moriarty
1787-1788	Richard Whatcoat, Sylvester Hutcheinson, John Cooper
1789	Lemuel Green, J. McClasky
1790	J. Robinson, S. Miller
1791	Lemuel Green, J. Robinson, S. Miller

At Boehms's Chapel

1792	John McClasky, Robert Cloud, Joseph Wainright
1793	Freeborn Garretson, William Hunter
1794	Valentine Cook, Isaac Robinson, Elijah Pelhem
1795	John Merrick, John Jarrell, Thomas Sargant, John Robinson
1796	Thomas Ware, Ephriam Chambers, James Stokes
1797	William Chandler
1798	William Chandler, Daniel Higby
1799	William Colbert, James Herron, Robert Benham, Edward Larkins
1800	Stephen Timmons, Richard Sneath, Thomas Jones
1801	William Hunter, Stephen Timmons, Robert McCoy
1802	William Hunter, John Bethell
1803	Anning Owen, William Brandon
1804	Henry Boehm
1805	John Osburn, J. Stephens
1806	Daniel Ireland
1807	Thomas Burch, W. H. Owen, J. Harmon

1808	Thomas Burch, John Miller
1809	John Walker, Thomas Miller, William Colbert
1810	James Bateman, John Walker
1811	H. Ross, R. Sparks
1812	James Saunders, James Mitchell, William Torbert
1813	R. Sneath, William Torbert, Thomas Evans
1814	Asa Smith, James Mitchess, James Sampson
1815	Thomas Miller, Phineas Price
1816	David Best, Thomas Miller
1817	Robert Burch, John Woolson
1818	R. Burch, P. Price, William Hunter
1819	William Leonard, J. Talley, William Hunter
1820	William Leonard, John Talley, William Hunter
1821	John Woolson, Henry King
1822	Henry Boehm, Joseph Holdich
1823	Henry Boehm, Wesley Wallace
1824	Jacob Gruber, James Moore, Thomas Miller
1825	Thomas Neal, George Wiltshire
1826	Henry Boehm, W. W. Wallace
1827	Henry Boehm, Daniel Parish
1828	George Wooley, John Nickelson
1829	George Wooley, T. M. Carroll
1830	David Best, N. Chew
1831	Eliphalet Reed, R. W. Thomas
1832	Thomas Miller, E. Reed, John Edwards
1833	W. Talbert, T. Millard
1834	W. Talbert, T. B. Tibblets
1835	J. N. Crane, T. B. Tibblets
1836	J. N. Crane, R. Anderson
1837	William Urie, Charles W. Jackson
1838	William Urie
1839	E. Kennard
1840	E. Kennard
1841	Gassoway Oran, Valentine Gay
1842	James Hand, Henry Atwater
1843	James Hand
1844	John Allen, Steven Patterson
1845	John Allen, William Montgomery
1846	William K. Gontner, William Montgomery
1847	William Gontner, J. B. McCullough
1848	E. Reed, J. Bissey
1849	E. Reed, J. Bissey
1850	James Smith, James Colder
1851	J. D. Curtis
1852	Charles Karsner, W. R. Robinson

1853	Valentine Day, J. B. Dennison
1854	V. Gray, A. Howard
1855	Henry Sutton, Mark Bailey
1856	William Major, J. B. Dennison
1857	William Major
1858	W. Walters
1859	W. Walters
1860	H. B. Manger
1861	W. B. Gregg, G. S. Shaffer
1862	W. B. Gregg
1863	J. Castle
1864	William Dairymope
1865	T. Montgomery
1866	J. E. Watson
1867-1869	J. E. Kessler
1870	J. Shields
1871-1872	H. B. Mauger
1873	J. Collins
1874-1875	S. G. Hare
1876-1878	F. M. Brady
1879-1881	J. W. Harkins
1882-1883	A. J. Amthor
1884	W. H. Smith
1885	Samuel Pancoust
1886-1887	F. G. Coxxon, C. W. Langley
1888	J. W. Perkinpine
1889	J. W. Wilson
1890-1893	C. S. Mervine
1894-1895	J. E. Deacon
1896	H. S. Beals
1897-1900	D. Gollie

At Boehm's Church

1901-1902	D. A. Hinkel
1903-1904	D. S. Sherry
1905	J. E. McVaugh
1906	H. B. Baird
1907-1910	William J. Lindsay
1911	Edward Divine
1912-1913	Ara W. Kauffman
1914-1917	Leo P. Zook
1918-1919	William H. Robinson
1920-1921	F. M. Clough
1922-1924	T. R. Crooks
1925-1927	James Hunt

1928-1933	Claude Grason
1934-1937	H. H. Truax
1938	G. L. Shaffer
1939-1940	John S. Smith
1941	H. F. Hamer
1941-1943	Abram W. Sangrey

APPENDIX B

Reminiscences of Lancaster Circuit - 1822

The text of this series of articles, written in 1878, by a Lancaster County Circuit Rider in 1822, is packed with unique, original reporting. Therefore it is transcribed in full. (Note the index references to Joseph Holdich in Boehm's *Reminiscences*.)

First Paper - June 6, 1878

I joined the Philadelphia Conference, held in old St. George's Church, in April, 1822. Bishop George presided. I was appointed to Lancaster Circuit with Rev. Henry Boehm, of precious memory.

The circuit embraced about the whole of Lancaster County, extending from the village of Coventry to within thirty-five miles of Philadelphia, and to Bainbridge, about fifteen miles from Harrisburg on the west. The extent was about fifty miles east to west, with about two hundred and fifty miles round, of the appointments.

We had about eight hundred members in society, with twenty-eight regular appointments, besides several occasional ones. Each of us preached on every round thirty-five times. It was a four-week circuit. The county was one of much wealth, but Methodism was comparatively feeble. We had to ford rivers, and slept often in uncomfortable homes. Many other places of entertainment were homes of comfort, and some of the best friends of my life were made there. In passing over Welsh Mountain we had to follow bridelpaths.

The circuit lay entirely within Lancaster County, having Lancaster city for its center. It embraced several quite important villages: among others, Columbia, Marietta, Bainbridge, Morgantown, Churchtown, Strasburg, Soudersburg, Springfield, and Coventry. And besides these we had numerous appointments in the rural parts, where we preached in school houses or private homes, as most convenient. In most of the villages which I have named we had churches, some of them quite good. There were also some important churches in the rural neighborhoods, among them one of the most interesting was known as Boehm's Chapel, located on the farm of Rev. Dr. (sic) Boehm,

father of the late Rev. Henry Boehm. The farm at that time was in the possession of the nephew, Mr. John Boehm, an excellent lay Methodist who later moved into Lancaster Village, where he lived until his decease, greatly respected. The Boehm home was one of the best "preachers homes" in the circuit.

Another of the pleasant appointments on the circuit was the "Swifts" who were a comfortable family there owning and occupying what was known as "Fulton House" being the very home in which Robert Fulton, the inventor, was born. In the present family (Swift) were six children, three sons and three daughters. Two of the sons, John and George, were particularly marked for their piety, zeal, and consistency. One of the daughters, familiarly and widely known as "Patty Swift" was more than usually gifted in prayer and exhortation, and was a universal favorite in the churches. At first we preached at Swift's house, but as a result of a good revival work there was built on a part of the Swift's farm a church during the year.

Another of the preaching places was at Mr. Schwartzwelder's, in a distant part of the circuit. Here also a chapel was built during the year. Among the memories associated with our preaching there was that of the following incident. During a revival meeting a young lady was among the seekers earnest in prayer. While thus engaged word was carried to her aunt with whom she resided, and the latter in great anger, hastened to the meeting and rushing forward to the prayer altar, seized her niece, and bore her in her arms towards the door. While doing so, the niece prayed more earnestly than ever, and before reaching the door was converted, and beginning to shout, her aunt dropped her, and in great trepidation ran from the building as though some strange apparition were in her wake.

Second Paper - June 20, 1878

As the city of Lancaster was the chief place on the circuit, it might be supposed that it was the place of most interest. This, however, was scarcely the case. There are many others remembered now with more pleasure. In that day Methodism was small and feeble. There were but two Methodist families of any consideration. These were Bonum Sampson and the Benedict family, worthy and excellent people. We also remember another character worthy of mention. He was an itinerant merchant, whose name I think was Kerr. He was a shrewd and intelligent person, with a remarkable gift in prayer. In many characteristics - in his intelligence, uprightness, and originality - he was not unlike the hero of Wordsworth's "Excursion". There was but one Methodist Church in the city - an unpretending brick building, perhaps forty or fifty feet in size. It was remarkable for a pulpit, under which a man of six feet could stand, thus raising the head of the preacher far above the level of the congregation.

While in this city we had a passing visit from the Lorenzo Dow, who preached in this church a plain and practical sermon from the text, "Then shall they fast in those days." Mark 2:20

As Lancaster was the head of the circuit it was also the residence of the senior preacher, Rev. Henry Boehm, whose house was my pleasant home while in that city. His character is too well known to need mention here. He was always like a father to the young preachers under his care. Mrs. Boehm was an inestimable woman, gentle, intelligent, and deeply pious, a perfect model for a minister's wife. She was of the respectable family of the Blackistons, on the eastern shore of Maryland. My heart always remembered her kindness to a raw and inexperienced youth.

Columbia was the second place of importance upon the circuit. It was ten miles from Lancaster, on the bank of the Susquehanna. Here we had a good and strong society, but worshipped in a small and uninviting building, which stood in an obscure part of the town, as was too often the custom in those early days.

Five miles above Columbia was Marietta. Here we preached in a school house to a small society, which like others we now understand has become firm and flourishing. As the building in which we worshiped was public property, it was found difficult to hold our meetings in private retirement. On one occasion a minister of another denomination remained for class meeting led by father Boehm. When he came to this stranger in his turn he asked his state of feeling, to which the clergyman replied he had no desire to speak upon that subject. Father Boehm gently replied, then I would say to you in the words of the apostle Peter "Be ready always to give an answer to any man that asketh you a reason of the hope that is in you, with meekness and fear - 1st Peter 3:15," and passed on to the next member.

We were frequently urged to extend our labors into

unoccupied places. In this way we were induced to visit Bainbridge, a village a few miles above Marietta. It was an unenlightened place. Here we established the first class-meeting ever found there. Composed of a few simple and earnest souls, among them the wife of a wealthy man who lived in a pleasant home near the village. She became effected by the views she heard preached and joined the Methodist Church, though opposed by her husband. But he too, through a providential accident, as he always thought, became a participant in her faith. On one occasion, following his wife to a camp-meeting, intending to frustrate if he could her religious purposes, he left his horse fastened and went on the ground. On returning he found that his animal had escaped and wandered off. After a long fruitless pursuit through the woods he returned and found the horse where he and originally tied him. This seemed to him so strange that he thought the finger of God was in it. It so effected him that he returned to the meeting, sought the Lord and professed conversion. He joined the church and remained faithful as long as his wife lived. After her death, however, he married a fashionable woman and became again a worldling.

On one occasion,during a prayer meeting in the place, a highly respected lady came forward and kneeled with other penitents at the altar. Someone carried word of this to their husband at this house. The news excited him greatly, and rushing to the church he seized her in his arms and carried her away. We were amazed, upon opening our eyes at the close of prayer and rising from our knees to find our penitent gone! I tell of this merely to show some of the character of the population at that time.

Third Paper - June 27, 1878

We resume our account of Methodism in Lancaster Circuit in 1822. Those who compare the present with the past might well exclaim "What hath God wrought!"

In connection with the appointments in the western part of the circuit, already mentioned were several occasional ones. Among them were Macurdys, Kings, Harts, Wrights, Martiques, and Millerstown; but there are places on the Minutes now which were quite unknown to us at that time. Among these for instance are Elizabethtown and Mount Joy.

At Strasburg, a village about eight miles from Lancaster, we had a strong and excellent society, though a small church edifice. The names of Connelly, Stacy, and

Groff may still be remembered. The brothers John and Abram Groff, were men whom it was a privilege to know. Valiant for the truth, fervent in prayer and abounding in hospitality, the tired preachers always found soothing welcomes in these families. Both were substantial farmers, living about a mile from Strasburg. John, the elder brother, was a local preacher. His household was permeated by the spirit of the gospel, and he lived upon an ample farm, which he enjoyed without personal labor. It was a rare and lovely spot. The cool spring that furnished the dairy issued from the cellar and supplied the pond from which was drawn fresh fish for the daily table, and the orchard near that supplied fruit for the celebrated Pennsylvania apple butter. It was a home enriched with the blessings of both worlds, and I must be pardoned for dwelling at length upon it in the connection, as after so many years it forms one of the sweetest memories of my life. The Groffs had married two sisters, both excellent women. Mrs. Abram Groff may have exceeded her sister mentally, but Mrs. John was the very embodiment of kindness, sincerity, and love. The weary ministers blessed her and thanked God for her cheering ministrations. When the very young minister was objected to on account of his youth, Mr. Groff took the risk; invited him to his home, and gave his name to a room which was always at this disposal afterwards whenever duty called him in that direction.

But it was not(!) through material instruments that Methodism reached its present level. Few "Bowers of ease" like Mr. Groff's awaited the preacher of these days. Methodism, like sunshine, shed its rays of light upon the lowliest places of the earth. One of our preaching places on this circuit was the house of a poor shoemaker, where worship was held in a small room, which served for meeting-room, eating-room, bed-room, workshop, and chapel in one. After preaching came the dinner, when the host took his wetstone from the bench, and after moistening it with his tongue, proceeded to sharpen the knives on the table, and, without further ceremony replaced them by the plates.

In those days quarterly meetings were great occasions. People, as is well known, came to them from all parts of the church; often from a distance of twenty, thirty, or forty miles, always expecting a season of religious interest and power. One of these was held at Strasburg that year, when some of the members desirous of showing respect to the Presiding Elder, Rev. James Bateman, requested the use of the large Lutheran Church for the sabbath service. It was granted, after the preaching in the evening was over a prayer-meeting was held in which penitents were invited forward for prayers. This was an unheard of thing in that church, and in disgust some of the leading members sent the organist to the gallery, who played marches and like music so loudly that the meeting had to be given up. The next day, a Methodists meeting, a member of the Lutheran Church, said to him, "What an excellent place yours is for getting sinners converted!" "Oh" the answer was, "we don't do such things in our church." Here we may remark, by the way, that on the day of our Strasburg appointment, after preaching and leading class in the morning, we rode three miles to preach and lead class at Soudersburg. From thence we rode twelve miles to preach at Lancaster at night.

This was done on every round of the circuit.

Fourth Paper - July 11, 1878

East of Lancaster is the town of New Holland, where we had neither church nor society but were requested to have worship in a private house near the town for the accommodation of a few families. On one occasion, it being harvest-time, we had an audience composed entirely of women, several of whom brought their dogs. The dogs got into a general fight, while we were at prayer, and we were obliged to suspend our exercises to bring them to order. Near this house was the small dwelling of a helpless invalid, whose request we carried the gospel to himself and a few neighbors who met at his house. At the village of Waynesburg, where we had no society, we preached at the house of Mr. Griffith, who was a substantial farmer and a Christian. The house of Thomas Hancock, a man of faith and prayer living in a retired situation at the foot of Welsh Mountain, was also opened for regular preaching to a small but attentive congregation.

Not to be too minute, we pass over several appointments recorded in an ancient memorandum book now soiled and defaced by time, to mention Harmony and Forest Meetinghouses then standing. At Morgantown we had no society, though we preached there at intervals. At Springfield, where the names of John and Elijah Bull may still be remembered, we had a good church. Father Boehm once preached there on "Prayer" and the next day, while proceeding on his circuit, was overtaken by an unknown gentleman who, accosting him abruptly, said "Sir, you did not state my speech correctly. I did not say that I would as soon as found robbing a hen roost as engaged in prayer." Father Boehm, in his courteous tones replied, "I have not the slightest idea of your meaning, sir. You are a perfect stranger to me." Oh, then, sir, I beg your pardon. I was mistaken" said the stranger; and they parted. This person proved to be a respected physician in the community. The next place to Springfield was Coventry, which was the extreme point on the circuit, where we had a substantial church and society. Among them I remember the names of Christman and Benjamin. Coventry finished our work at the eastern end of the circuit.

Returning now towards Lancaster, the enabled persons to compare the past with the present we simply name our several appointments: Jacob High's, Thomas Millard's, Trago's, Schwartzwelder's, S. Townsend's, and Steward's. During that year we held a very interesting Camp-meeting near Churchtown, a place already mentioned, at which much good was done. It was remarkable for revivals of religion,that extended to Trago's and Schwartzwelder's. In the latter place it was followed by an increase of members and issued in the building of a new church called at that time Sadsbury Meetinghouse; now I believe Asbury Church. In this place we answer a query proposed to us by Rev. G. W. Lybroad, historiographer of the Philadelphia Conference, at whose suggestions these papers were undertaken. It is whether the town of Reading was at that time in the Lancaster circuit or not. It was not, but was introduced there the succeeding year in the following manner. On our circuit were two zealous and enterprising young men named Emmon Kimber and Samuel Pettit. Their business led them to Reading, where Methodism was unknown and were there existed a state of perfect religious apathy. Seeing the need of more spiritual influence in the place, they invited the preachers of the Lancaster Circuit to establish worship there, securing a schoolhouse for that use. Here preaching was commenced with the usual results. Some lawless young men, out of derision, appointed a prayer meeting as a travesty of the newly arrived Methodists. In profane mockery they invited persons to a mourner's bench, at which a young man knelt and with them offered derisive prayers. He continued motionless, however, for some time after they became quiet, and on going to him they found him dead. The circumstances caused as great a shock in Reading as a somewhat similar one did in the Apostolic Church, where "great fear came upon as many as heard these things." This put an end to all opposition to Methodism in Reading, which from that time went on successfully. this incident has been related to me several times and confirmed by undoubted witnesses who knew all the facts. [cf: Henry Boehm Reminiscences p. 109!]

Fifth Paper - July 18, 1878

Having now concluded the relation of incidents in Lancaster Circuit, a few remarks of a more general nature will close this series of papers. In the old memorandum book before referred to, we find the following statement: This A.D. 1822-23 from May 26 to April 27, have preached 327 times, met in class about 800 members each round of the circuit; rode about 3,000 miles; spent $137 59¼; received into society, 377; lost by removal, death and expulsion, 150; leaving an increase of 227."

In explanation of this small expenditure, we may remark that we have nothing to pay for board, as this was given gladly by our good member. There were some powerful revivals of religion during this year from which sprung several of the churches already mentioned.

It may interest the readers to hear of the preachers with whom we were most familiar at that time. The first we name is James Bateman, our Presiding Elder. He was much above the average of the brethren, a man of superior culture, amiable disposition pleasing manners and fine nature. He was an excellent preacher, thoughtful, tender, graceful, and often in manner extremely effective, though his eloquence penetrated like the dew rather than swept like the storm. He inspired strong, personal attachments. I remember a warm friend of his praising him extravagantly to a superficial young lady who did not know him personally, and who said after being introduced to brother Bateman: "I saw nothing remarkable about him except an uncommonly white cravat." "Oh" replied his friend, "his soul is as white as his cravat." One day in the street a fashionable looking lady, on passing him, said to her companion in a scornful tone, loud enough for him to hear, "Is that one of their great preachers?" Turning back to her he answered quietly, mildly, no doubt to her great confusion, "No, madam, I make no pretension to being a great preacher. You must have mistaken me for some other person." Then quietly pursued his way.

Jacob Gruber, of eccentric memory, was another striking character of that day. Of him, as another it may be quaintly said, that "he gained knowledge less by studies than by prayer." So much has been said of this good man's peculiarities, that other points of his character have been lost sight of. He was a man of strong natural sense, of deep emotion, and ernest convictions. He was deeply pious, zealous, and devoted to his work. His preaching abounded in wit and sarcasm, often very telling and not infrequently it melted into pathos causing tears to mingle with the smiles of his hearers. He might be considered the Hugh Latimer of Methodism. He was far from being a methodical sermoniser. His discourses were practical and hortatory, abounding in evangelical truth. He did not deal in protracted argument, but generally put his reasoning in a pithy and programmatic form. For instance he once said: "Some people who deny the doctrine of Christian perfection still hold a higher perfection than the Methodists do, for they believe that a person can become so perfect that he cannot fall."

Once preaching on the perseverance of the saints, he said, "Some people think that when a soul is converted, he is not as safe as if he were already in heaven, with the door locked and the key lost." In these days of tight lacing, large bonnets, and flounces, he compared fashionable ladies to "wasps, small in the middle and big at both ends." Once in a country church he quoted I John 3:2, from a Bible deficient in leaves, "And now we are the *children* of God" when a young minister sitting near to Gruber audibly corrected him by saying "Sons, brother." "Yes, but I did not want to leave the sisters out" he quietly replied. Such chance utterances give us a better idea, perhaps, of the character of the man and his times than a more labored description.

It will be most ungrateful of me in listing the preachers of that day, to omit Henry G. King, for he was my spiritual father. Without any pretensions of learning or graceful oratory, he was a sound, practical and energetic preacher. His sermons abounded in scriptural truth and deep Christian experience, while the ardor of his soul sometime gave extravagance to his manner. He was a man might in prayer, and very uniform and constant in his devotions.

His sweetness of disposition and kindness of spirit endeared him to all. He lived eminently near to heaven. I remember that one time during a protracted illness a member of the family with whom he stayed said it was "a privilege to have him in their house, like having an angel in the family." He was remarkably cheerful in spirit and conversation, and interested in both the old and the young. On one occasion I remember that some persons, in speaking to the Eastern Shore of Maryland, dwelt upon the fervent piety of the people, and also upon the hospitality and good cheer. A gentleman present said that was true, but that it was a very sickly region, and that preachers were not apt to live long there. Brother King replied, "O, what can we utter; the best of piety here, the best of worldly cheer, and early death, and heaven hereafter forever."

Of all my earliest associations in the ministry, no name is more dear to me then that of Henry Grubb King.

Before closing these recollections of Lancaster Circuit, it might be interesting to note the difference of the condition of the Methodist Church then and now. In all this region there was not a single Sunday School, Bible Class, Bible, Tract or Missionary Society. Scriptural and experimental religion was a new thing among the people who were generally profoundly ignorant on the subject of religion, needing instructions in the first elements. As an illustration we may relate a conversation that occurred near the Forest Meetinghouse. Some men were talking on the recent death of a neighbor, and one said "He died a Methodist." The other said "O, I don't believe that" "Well, rejoined the first, "At any rate he sent for Jonathan Bull" a local preacher already mentioned, "to talk and pray with him." "O, I don't believe that. I guess, rather, he died a believer." This came to me from unquestioned sources.

Little was thought of, by the ministers and Christian people of those days, but the immediate awakening and conversion of sinners. The outward applications of religion were not much attended to. It was not until the Methodists became more numerous and enlightened that Sunday Schools, Bible-classes and the like, combined with the preaching was felt. Hence it was said, and not without truth, that the Methodists in that day were far more successful in the conversion of sinners than in the building up of believers.

Still, there were many highly intelligent as well as

deeply pious persons among us, whose influence for good was certainly felt. Through them and through a more highly educated and better trained class of ministers, Methodism, without losing its power and its fervor, has not only greatly increased in number, but likewise attained a vastly higher level than it had reached in my early days on Lancaster Circuit.

As it has been there, so it has been in the Methodist Church generally, proving that the influence of the Bible and of true Christianity must inevitably advance the interests of society and civilization.

Written By: Joseph Holdich, D.D. Morristown, NJ, June 17, 1878.

(Transcribed from the *New York Christian Advocate* files at Old St. George's Church, Philadelphia, May 10, 1985.)

APPENDIX C

Boehm's Church Records Inventory

A small amount of old, original church-records material exists on Boehm's Church. As with so many local churches, (1) there was probably not a strong incentive or desire in favor of permanent record keeping by the early members; and (2) if records were made, they have not been kept or preserved for posterity. Some have probably been lost, and (3) there is no existing report of inventory which might account for the first, extant records there. And no careful inventory of existing records has been made.

The following is an inventory of the Boehm's Church Records.

A. The oldest extant records of the Boehm's Church appears in a "Boehm's Circuit" record book, in an old volume titled "Minutes Of The Safe Harbor Circuit Quarterly Conference," March 1852 to December 26, 1868. It includes Boehm's along with the other stations on the circuit.

This precious book should be promptly reproduced for preservation by xerox or microfilm, before it is further deteriorated or faded. (It will be useful in the writing of the History Of The Boehms United Methodist Church!) It is presently filed with the archives and history materials at the Conestoga UMC.

Quarterly Conference, (first, second, third, fourth) was a gathering of representative members from each of the "station" churches on the "circuit" to transact business, hear reports, including the pastor's report, conducted by the Presiding Elder. In today's terms it was a combination of official board and charge conference business. The circuit included Boehms, Conestoga, Marticville, Millersville, Safe Harbor, Washington Boro.

B. The second extant collection of original, old Boehm's Church records - again as part of the Boehm's Circuit - covers the period 1866-1888, consisting of these sections: Pastors; Official Members; Classes; Probationers; Members In Full; Marriages; Baptisms. These records also are in the keeping of the Conestoga UMC.

Fortunately, xerox copies were made of these, many pages of old records, in a preservation and education project originating with Ms. Pauline James Eshelman, in

April 1983; and copies are available on file at Conestoga and at Lancaster County Historical Society. It certainly would behoove the Boehm's UMC board to take two actions: (1) to obtain xerox copies of these old record-book pages; and (2) to prepare an index of the Boehm's names from these pages. (Ms. Eshelman, who was motivated in this most commendable preservation project because of her family relationships at the Conestoga Church, has set the precedent by her indexing of the Conestoga congregation's names section.)

C. Thirdly, the following historic record books and materials are preserved at the Boehm's UMC, in these categories: (1) Class Meeting Attendance Record Books, 1861-1877. (2) Membership Record Book, 1897-1950; and more recently edited membership records. (3) An assortment of Minutes record books, during this 20th century, Quarterly Conference, Official Board, and Charge Conference Meetings. (4) An assortment of programs and brochures, pictures, and memorabilia of anniversary and special days. (5) The church files contain substances of records and information about the life and work of the present congregation and its mission, including copies of Sunday Bulletins, Newsletters, etc.

APPENDIX D
A Citation To Alan Holliday

In the thought that the words of this citation do gather up commendation to Mr. Holliday, they also embody the early spirit of restoration at Boehms Chapel, and are therefore recorded here as a part of that history.

Whereas, progeny in the "land of the children of Wesley" of faithful parents, your father a pastor in America - you understand the language of the faith and practice of Christian discipleship; and

Whereas, the style of your life lets you hear it said: "One to whom much is given, of him shall much be required" (Lk. 12:48) you have answered "yes" to the community and in every church, when friends and pastors and bishops have asked you to help; and

Whereas, typically bearing the highest honors: at work, as President of the International Association of Printing Craftsmen; in the community, the YMCA's Master Of Men Award; in your church, variously as Lay Leader, Annual Conference Lay Member, Chairman of the Board of Managers Cornwall Manor, and

Whereas, you see in every personal relationship opportunities for inspiring self-confidence and hope in others, your friends and fellow workers - relationships that often move in confidence, and strength, and human kindness, and generosity, and

Whereas, you have brought these same professional and personal qualities an immeasurable contribution to the project of preservation and restoration of historic Boehm's Chapel - where, with friends there, your commitment and leadership have helped fashion an organization and develop permanent artifacts which will assure its proper place in our archives and history, and

Whereas, your dedication of time, and talent, and resources, your wise counsel and enthusiastic support, your faith and concern - these things have been an example and inspiration for others - and at the same time it is fun to work with you.

THEREFORE, be it RESOLVED that we, members of the Boehm's Chapel Committee, you serving as chairperson from 1975 to 1982 - and now as the mantle and work of that Committee passes to the Boehm's Chapel Society - do express our warm thanks and sincere appreciation to you...(with these signatures attached...) - June 1982.

APPENDIX E

A Commendation for the *Reminiscences*

There is another priceless section of the *Reminiscences* which deserves, verbatim so appropriately to be included in this writing.

(I struggled in the layout whether perchance to include it in Chapter 2. It is added here for those readers who may miss obtaining a personal copy of the *Reminiscences*!)

Five pages, 494-499, introduce the 100-page addition to the first, 1865 edition of the great book, written by its editor and Henry Boehm's biographer, Rev. Dr. J. B. Wakeley. It is the best, brief written sketch of Henry's life, plus a dramatic 21-line description of how the *Reminiscences* was composed. I predict these pages will be used as the introduction, when and if a modern best-seller biography of Henry Boehm is published. It is absolutely appropriate to be included here.

History And Nature Of Father Boehm's Reminiscences - The Last Ten Years Of His Life

Father Boehm's valuable life has been marvelously prolonged to such a very old age that he is now regarded every-where, in Europe and America, as the patriarch of Methodism, and so many interests cluster around the aged veteran that we add a few chapters to his Reminiscences.

There are several classes of men. There are those who live wholly in the past, others live wholly in the present, and others wholly in the future. These are all in the wrong.

The man who lives with an eye on the past, the present, and the future; who looks backward, and forward, and around him; who makes the past tell on the present, the present on the future - he is the live man; he understands the true philosophy of life; he will accomplish the most good, and secure the greatest happiness. The inspired penman says: "Inquire, I pray thee, of the former age, and prepare thyself to the search of their fathers: (for we are but of yesterday, and know nothing:)...shall not they teach thee, and tell thee, and utter words out of their heart?"

The reader will readily see why we add a few chapters to the original volume. "Boehm's Reminiscences, Historical

and Biographical," as one of the richest volumes in Methodist literature. It is remarkable, first, for the antiquity of its contents, taking us back to the origin of American Methodism: second, for its originality; the old gentleman drew upon his own resources; there has never been any thing like it, and it is doubtful whether there ever will be again; in it he testifies what he has seen and heard, and he has seen much, for he has lived a great many years: third, for the description he gives for men and things, and the simplicity of its style: fourth, for its facts; he never gives wings to his imagination; on the contrary, he deals in sober history and truthful biography. Had it been written in another style it would not have been his, for he is a plain, matter-of-fact man; he stated truth in its simplest form, without any embellishment.

In his volume there are no false colorings,no exaggerations; it is true to nature and true to life. All honor to the truthful veteran who introduces to us so many of the heroes of Methodism, whose names and fame are immortal! He presents before his readers Robert Strawbridge, the apostle of Methodism in Maryland; Dr. Thomas Coke, the founder of modern missions, whose heart was large enough to hold four continents,and who found a grave in the Indian Ocean; what a graphic description he gives of Jesse Lee, the apostle of Methodism to New England, and the first historian of American Methodism! We hear him preach his last sermons, and these were delivered in God's great cathedral - nature's magnificent temple; we are taken into the chamber of the dying saint; we see Father Boehm wetting the parched lips of the dying hero, smoothing his pillow of agony, speaking words of cheer; we see him kneel down by his bedside and commend the dying one to Him who is "the resurrection and the life;" we hear a shout of joy from the dying one; we see him as his breath grows shorter and shorter, till he heaves one long, deep-drawn sigh, and all is over; we see Boehm with his own hands close his eyes and put the muffler around his face; we see the open grave, and Father Boehm laying him quietly to rest. Sleepless nights, restless days, watching, waiting, trembling, hoping, till all was over. What affection, what care, what solicitude, what unwavering faith, what ardent love!

He introduces us to Bishop Whatcoat, that seraphic man. We have a description of his person, of his preaching, of his last sickness, and his triumphant death. He gives the best description of Bishop Asbury ever written; and no man ever knew him better, for he was with him in the closet intimacy for five years. We have a description of his person, his dress. We have Asbury in the family, Asbury in the pulpit, Asbury in the conferences, Asbury among friends, Asbury among strangers, Asbury among the children. He describes so vividly the bishop's sermons and exhortations we imagine we see and are listening to the great apostle of American Methodism. O how graphic is Boehm's description of Bishop Asbury!

In regard to the volume, let me say, it was prepared with the greatest care. For years we were employed on it at different intervals. We took his own journals and read them carefully; then we read Asbury's journals to refresh his mind; then we questioned him concerning men and places, and in regard to General and Annual Conferences. We took down, from his "own lips," anecdotes and incidents till we were sure there was not one left. The work was complete; it was finished; the stock was exhausted. Not an original idea but we had obtained not an anecdote but we have recorded it. We never stopped pumping till the water was out of the well. There is no chance to glean over the fields we passed over, for we not only gathered the grain, but we gleaned as we went along. We never could get the old veteran to say what he did not distinctly remember. We might ask him over and over again, "Did not such a thing take place? Were you not there?" "*I do not remember*," was the emphatic answer. After the chapters were written we read them over to him, and he appended the following to each: -

"This chapter is correct. Henry Boehm."

Note: Each chapter was dated at the place where it was written. Some were written in New York, others in Harlem, still others in Yonkers, Poughkeepsie, and other places.

It is ten years since the first edition of this volume was published. Since that time Father Boehm has enjoyed a peaceful old age. He has visited an Annual Conference occasionally, where he has been an object of great attention.

He visited his own Conference, Philadelphia, which he joined in 1801, and his visit was as welcome as if he had been an angel from heaven. Its members hung upon the lips of the old Methodist patriarch in silent wonder as he described the fathers who had fallen asleep, and the early days and scenes in which he was such a prominent actor, and then drew a contrast between the past and present, showing how Methodism had advanced. He was an object of great interest at the great Centenary Meeting in the city of New York, at Cooper Institute, in October 1866, Daniel Ross, Esq., presiding. Rev. Thomas Sewall, D.D., delivered one of the most eloquent addresses I ever listened to. The venerable Boehm was on the platform, and his appearance gave additional charm to the intensely interesting meeting. In the midst of his address, replete with beauty, abounding in historical reminiscences, the speaker turned to Father Boehm, and delivered a personal address to him. He said: "We thank you, venerable father, for lingering so long among us to cheer us by your presences, your example and for giving us so many interesting reminiscences of the past. Thou art a representative of the former age of Methodism - thou art a splendid representative of the fathers. Venerable man, friend of Coke and Asbury, Whatcoat and M'Kendree, we thank you for your presence here; you are the great link that connects the past with the present."

After invoking many blessings on his head, and a glorious future, he concluded his address of beauty, eloquence, and power, one that will not soon be forgotten. Now his voice is silent in death.

Father Boehm has of late years led such a quiet life that there are few additional reminiscences, or anecdotes to record. He is a grand specimen of religion in old age. His days glide on, calm and peaceful as a summer evening. The autumn of life is peculiarly beautiful in him. It is charming to see grace thrive, when nature decays; while the outer man is perishing, to see the inner man renewed day by day in vigor, in knowledge, in joy. It is delightful to see his fading eye brighten at the promise, "Where I am, there shall also my servant be;" to see his aged, wrinkled countenance glow with seraphic beauty.

Happy, happy old man! splendid specimen of the venerated fathers. He has "fought the good fight," he has "kept the faith," and will soon "finish his course." The past, the present, and the future smiled upon him. It will soon be said concerning him: "Servant of God, well done!/ Thy Glorious warfare's past; / The battle's fought, the race is won, / And thou art crown'd at last".

APPENDIX F

Some Boehm's Property Transactions

The 1943 writing Appendix included a transcription of Boehm's original Property Deed. That priceless copy has since been laminated and thus (more or less) permanently preserved. It is among the Boehm's Collection. It need not, therefore, appear in this writing. But among some other documents reproduced in 1943, (including the Church Incorporation Papers) a brief of some early property transactions does seem worth printing here.

On November 11, 1898, H. F. Eshelman, attorney-at-Law, prepared a brief of the titles to the Boehms property as far as it appeared of record.

The title to the Boehms property as far as it appears of record is as follows:

1750 Jacob Beam and Barbara his wife to Martin Beam. Deed Mar. 26, 1750 for 181 acres of land in Pequea Township, then a part of Conestoga.

This was a part of the tract of land that the Boehms tract now consists of.

1761 Proprieties of Pennsylvania - Penn and others to Martin Beam. Patent form the grantors dated 14 Oct. 1761 for 102 acres of land in Pequea Twp. and 144 perches. Recorded in Pat. Book at Phil. AA Vol. 2. p. 45.

1765 Jacob Stoner and Wife to Martin Beam. Deed dated June 28, 1765 for 21 acres in Pequea Twp. recorded in Book L. p. 167.

These three tracts of land were adjoining and the Boehms tract was made upon parts of the three. It seems to lie where they come together.

1783 Martin Beam and Wife to Jacob Beam. Deed dated 21 June 1783, recorded in Book NN. p. 387 being a tract of 273 acres, a part of the three above combined tracts and the tract out of which the Boehms tract was taken.

1824 Jacob Beam to John Gyer and Martin Beam Jr. Trustees. Deed Dated Nov. 20, 1824 recorded in Book C No. 5, p. 200 a tract of 261 acres of land in Pequea Twp. among others in trust to sell the same for the said grantor etc. and with power to give deeds. A part of the above.

1825 Martin Beam and John Gyer assignees and trustees of Jacob Beam to John Beam. Deed dated Apr. 4, 1825 for

261 acres of land in Pequea Twp. same as the above tract, recorded in Book K. Vol. 6 p. 147 being the tract out of which the Boehms tract was sold.

1856 Dr. Jacob Heiss executor of Will of John Beam to Henry Hess. Deed dated Nov. 3, 1856, recorded in book O. Vol. 8, 270 for a tract of land containing 200 acres more or less, in Pequea Twp. being tract out of which the Boehms tract was sold, under power in will of John Boehm. Charges with a dower in favor of widow of John Beam of $5000.

In fall of 1862 the widow died and Oct. 1, 1862 the legatees of John Beam - Dr. Heiss and Mrs. Hess released the $5000 dower, recorded in Book E. Vol. 9, p. 570. That makes the title clear at this point.

1867 Henry Hess and Wife to Samuel Charles, Pequea. Deed Mar. 29, 1867 recorded in Book O. Vol. 9, 159, for a farm in Pequea Twp. of 138 acres and out of which Sam. Charles's Admrs. sold the Boehms tract.

This is the end of the recorded title at this date - Nov. 11, 1898.

APPENDIX G

Old Blue Leaflet

Boehm's chapel

LANCASTER COUNTY PENNSYLVANIA

SYMBOL
OF THE
UNITED METHODIST CHURCH

1791

Location: Along Rt. 272, one mile south of Willow Street, Pa

A PROGRAM OF PRESERVATION AND RESTORATION
BY

THE
BOEHM'S CHAPEL SOCIETY

Designed and printed by Science Press
Methodist Bicentennial, 1984

The Spirit of God was moving in America in the years 1765-1815. Four pioneers of this spiritual movement were Francis Asbury, Philip William Otterbein, Martin Boehm, and Jacob Albright. If it is possible to locate a single area which focuses their most intense spiritual experiences, and if there is an area where they were associated more often in Divine leadership and power, that one place is Lancaster County. This is truly an exciting historic fact. And if there is a site within the area which symbolizes that movement, that site is Boehm's Chapel, the first structure built for Methodist worship in Lancaster County.

See the dates along that 50-year period spotted here to show something of the nature of that movement. Space allows only some of the dates and events; we hope enough to give a picture of the time and place.

Boehm's Chapel (1791) is the fourth oldest existing structure

MARTIN BOEHM (upper left) FRANCIS ASBURY (upper right)
PHILLIP W. OTTERBEIN (lower left) JACOB ALBRIGHT (lower right)

BOEHM'S CHAPEL
MARTIN BOEHM
1725–1812

His father, Jacob, a blacksmith-farmer, landed at Philadelphia, 1715, went to the Mennonite Pequea settlement, and married Barbara Kendig. Martin born 1725 built house in 1750, and married Eva Steiner (Stoner, in 1753.

1756 Chosen by lot and called as a minister among the Society of Mennonites.

1759 Succeeded Mennonite Bishop Jacob Hostetter and began work of spiritual shepherd to area congregations, including Byerland. He was to become involved in a new spiritual movement.

His own house and barn became a place of public worship. Those who came early to this place included Robert Strawbridge, organizer in Maryland of the first Methodist Society in America 1760s, Richard Webster, William Thomas, Benjamin Abbott, Richard Whatcoat, Thomas Ware, William Colbert, Jessee Lee, and Francis Asbury.

1767 Preaching at LONG'S BARN. (see under Otterbein)

1783 Sold all but one of his three farms to his sons—we infer, from a felt need he had to give more time to preaching.

1791 BOEHM's CHAPEL is built. Its architecture is contemporary, with simple rectangular lines 32 x 40 feet; thick lime stone walls; a balcony lined three sides; a high pulpit ascended by stairs distinguished the chancel; broad-board floors.

"My brother Jacob gave the land for the Chapel and the burying ground. It was called Boehm's Chapel because it was built upon Boehm's land in Boehm's neighborhood, and because the different families did much towards its erection, and were regular attendants."
—Henry Boehm, Journal

". . . in trust to and for the use of the Religious Society of Protestants in and near the said township of Conestoga called Methodists, for the purpose of erecting churches, Meeting Houses and Houses of Religious Worship and School Houses and burying grounds for the said religious Society called Methodists."
—original land deed—extant

The building plans were probably developed by Richard Whatcoat appointed itinerant Elder of the circuit and later bishop.

1812 Martin Boehm is dead.

Henry said of his preaching, "He preached with great life and power, and success."

United Brethren Church historian Phares Gibble states (1951), "The contribution of Father Boehm to the evangelical movement in general and the United Brethren in Christ church in particular cannot be overstated. His breaking away from established order and precedent, his overwhelming power over the gainsayer, his evangelical passion and resolute persuasiveness, stamp him as a man of exceptional moral purpose and extraordinary spiritual gifts. The spiritual reformation he wrought was nothing short of revolutionary in character."

1775 Henry Boehm born. Youngest son of Martin and Eve. One of eight children.

1798 Henry's religious awakening. While living with brother Jacob he led nearby Soudersburg Class. Here a church was built 1802.

1802 Henry received on trial in the Methodist Conference.

1804 Henry's journal while traveling the Dauphin Circuit tells of developing relationships: "We held what were called union or friendly meetings, where the Methodists and the United Brethren in Christ met in harmony, and the ministers took turns in preaching. These meetings were of great interest to the Methodists. It gave them access to many they could not otherwise have reached. We held one of these meetings in Columbia in August. Multitudes were present. James Thomas preached the first sermon, then my father preached in German, then I preached in English. Thus we had three sermons in the forenoon without intermission. In the afternoon three of the United Brethren (preached) . . ."

1807 Henry assisting in first translation into German of the Methodist Discipline.

1808 Henry, appointed to travel with Bishop Asbury, says, ". . . he was sixty-three years old when I began . . . and I traveled with him much longer than any of his other companions . . ."

FRANCIS ASBURY 1745–1816.

Appointed by Britain's John Wesley declaring, "our brethren in America call aloud for help" (1771). For the next 45 years as its foremost Methodist organizer and its first bishop he earned the title, "The Prophet of the Long Road." His successful insistence on the principle of "itinerancy" and his network of "Methodist Circuit Riders" became a pattern for all groups whose ministry kept pace with the advancing frontier, including the United Brethren and the Evangelical Churches.

1783 Bishop Francis Asbury first visited and preached at Boehm's. Nearly every year thereafter for 35 years he found Boehm's a resting place, ". . . where he answered letters and refitted for his long journeys."

Evangelical Church historian Raymond Albright likens the movement of these pioneers, at the close of the 18th Century, unto the great Protestant Reformation. (nearly three centuries earlier) ". . . on a somewhat smaller scale, we see that men like Asbury, Otterbein, Boehm, and Albright called the attention of their contemporaries to the true nature of religion, its very close and practical relation with all aspects of living, and in half a century won thousands to a religious experience which was intellectually valid, richly colored with emotional appeal, and morally controlling."

1815 Bishop Asbury's last visit to Boehm's. Touching parting scene with Henry at King and Charlotte Streets, Lancaster.

PHILIP W. OTTERBEIN 1726–1813.

1752 Came to America. Pastor German Reformed Church Lancaster. Background of scholarship combined with life-long emphasis on peitism—Bible reading, confession, free prayer, hymn singing, testimony of personal religious exprience—Biblical faith seen as life commitment to God.

1767 LONG'S BARN. At a "great meeting" held in the barn and orchard of Isaac Long, Lancaster Co. When Martin Boehm finished preaching Otterbein arose, embraced him and exclaimed "we are brethren." Here was the spiritual birth of the United Brethren in Christ Church.

1773 Pastor of Baltimore separatist German Evangelical Reformed Church, until his death.

1800 Otterbein and Martin Boehm appointed overseers or bishops at the organizing conference of United Brethren, in Maryland.

1813 Ordained three United Brethren elders, an incident very like the ordination by Anglican John Wesley of two elders for the Methodist ministry in America.

JACOB ALBRIGHT 1759–1808.

Confirmed a Lutheran. Settled in Lancaster Co.

1791 Religious awakening came during a prayer meeting in the house of a United Brethren family. Became a lay preacher with the Methodist Episcopal Church.

1807 Ordained in 1803 to leadership in the Evangelical society; and elected Bishop in 1807.

1784 America's Methodist Episcopal Church founded. Asbury and Coke designated superintendents (bishops).

1922 The Evangelical Association became known as The Evangelical Church.

1946 The United Brethren and The Evangelical Church merged into The Evangelical United Brethren Church.

1968 The Methodist Church and The Evangelical United Brethren Church merged to become The United Methodist Church.

erected for Methodist use in the U.S.A.—the other three being, Barratt's Chapel (1780), Acuff's Chapel (1786), and Rehoboth Church (1786). More important though is its uniqueness in time and events in the history of the evangelical movement which came together in the United Methodist Church 1968. Boehm's Chapel is a physical symbol of the merger.

What it was that made the reunion of our churches so very right and urgent in 1968 can be identified with the Spirit and power of that movement indigenous to Lancaster County, PA in the 18th Century—more than any other region in America.

Boehm's Chapel was "improved." In **1883** the galleries were removed, the old high pulpit was taken out, the gallery windows masoned shut, the ceiling lowered, and new benches were made. This "improved" condition is what we have inherited. But this needs to be preserved. Preserved, that is, as we get ready to **restore** Boehm's Chapel to its **1791 condition.** Restoration is the ultimate goal.

The Boehm's Chapel Society was founded to preserve and restore Boehm's Chapel, enhance understanding and appreciation of our heritage, and inspire the present generations. We hope that you will join the Society, and contribute to the restoration of Boehm's Chapel.

Boehm's Chapel is recognized as a historical site by the United Methodist Church, the Lancaster County Historic Preservation Trust, and the Pennsylvania Historical Commission. It will likely be designated a Methodist shrine in 1984.

SOURCES AND NOTES

[1] *The History Of Boehms Methodist Church*, Willow Street, Lancaster County, Pa., 1791-1943. Bachelor Of Divinity Degree Dissertation, the Theological Seminary, Evangelical and Reformed Church, Lancaster, Pa. by Abram W. Sangrey, May, 1943. Unpublished thesis.

An interesting aside: as per the accustomed procedure, a studied dissertation is printed in three copies, one going to the library of the primary institution; sometime in the mid-1950s a District Superintendent while visiting Boehm's Church "borrowed" this institution copy of the History and failed to return it - the copy then thought and reported to be lost. In 1980 it was discovered in the "Boehm's UMC" file-collection at the Conference Archives Center, Philadelphia, placed there by the family of the (now deceased) D.S.'s son who, of course, had no knowledge of the "lost" restricted copy!

[2] See: *How To Write A Local Church History*, by Frederick E. Maser, The Commission On Archives and History, UMC, Madison, NJ, 1989.

[3] Boehm, Rev. Henry, Reminiscences, Historical and Biographical, Of Sixty-four Years in the Ministry. Edited by Joseph B. Wakeley. (New York, Carlton and Porter) 1875. p. 579.

[4] His sources cited: Lednum's Rise Of Methodism In America; Henry Boehm's Reminiscences; Asbury's Journal; Drury's Life Of The Rev. Philip Otterbein; and Steven's History Of the Methodist Episcopal Church.

[5] This *History Of The Boehm (Beam) Family*, written by M. Stanley Boehm and Donald C. Beam, was excerpted from a 10-page mimeographed copy, obtained from a member of the family in 1985. Also received at the same time was a xeroxed copy of *A History Of The Beam Family* (with similar history) written in 1919 by Prof. Jacob Beam, of Princeton. NOTE: At the time of this writing, it is reported that Boehm's Chapel associates, James and Dorothy Galloway, of Columbus, Ohio, (descendants of the Boehm family) are researching for publication a genealogical Boehm family history.

[6] Rem. p. 579.

[7] Rem. p. 495.

[8] Rem. p. 499.

[9] Rem. p. 438ff.

[10] Rem. p. 480-485.

[11] Rem. p. 484-488.

[12] Rem. p. 494-587.

[13] Rem. p. 496.

[14] Bishop Francis Asbury and The Rev. Henry Boehm, by George L. Heiges, Lancaster County Historical Society. Lancaster, Pa. Journal Vol. 70 No. 3, 1966 p. 129-162.

[15] National Methodist Campmeeting At Manheim in 1868, by George L. Heiges. Vol. 43, 1943. Historical Society, Lancaster, Pa. p. 10-12.

[16] Rem. p. 30.

[17] See: The First Methodist Society In America, An Historical Inquiry; by H. K. Carroll (one of the Commissioners) Published by the Methodist Historical Society of The City Of New York, 1916. See also: How Methodism Came - The Beginnings of Methodism In America, by Ruthella Mary Bibbins, Second Abridged Edition; Strawbridge Shrine Association, Baltimore, Md. 1987.

[18] Rem. p. 113.

[19] Rem. p. 19-29.

[20] On April 8, 1991, a copy of this rare, original photograph of the 1791 Chapel was offered to the writer by Mr. and Mrs. Claude Hart, historians at Mt. Hope UMC. It is the only, known photograph of this image in existence! We do not know the picture's origin. We guesstimate this photo was made around 1875. The chapel's apparent, visible run-down condition here, implies that time when it was "reopened" for use. Copies from the printer's engraving

have been reproduced endlessly. This picture will be placed with the Boehm's Collection, in a frame fashioned from 200-year-old floor joists from the old chapel floor.

[21] Rem. p. 29.

[22] Rem. p. 113.

[23] Rem. p. 186ff.

[24] Rem. p. 372ff.

[25] As part of the EPCs, Lancaster District, UMC 1984 Centennial, a project designed to place roadmarkers at a selected group of eight historic sites in the County was developed. The other seven include: Reinholdsville Church, Blanesport; Soudersburg Church, Lincoln Highway East; Newcomer's Birthplace, Bareville; the Christian Grosh House, New Holland; the Jacob Albright Farm, Fryville; John Seybert Birthplace, Manheim. (These and other renowned UMC locations in Lancaster County will be highlighted in an upcoming history to be published on the UMC in Lancaster County.) The placement of the "official" PA marker at Boehms Chapel was also a concurrent project in 1984.

[26] See Appendix No. 2 for a unique, 1878, series of articles written on the Lancaster Circuit in 1822.

[27] See Appendix No. 3 for a Boehm's Church Records Inventory.

[28] See Appendix cited in [27] above.

[29] See History '43. p. 75.

[30] Readers should note the slightly different words used, explaining the reason(s) for undertaking the "improvements" from an article released, by the same pastor, to the *New York Christian Advocate, November 29, 1883*, which said: **Boehm's Chapel, located six miles south of Lancaster, Pa., in the Philadelphia Conference, is one of the venerable landmarks of the Methodism. Built in 1791, its walls echoed the preaching of Asbury and other pioneer itinerants. It is a small stone structure, and its**

interior has long presented a strange appearance. A paneled gallery extended around three sides, nearly covering the first floor. At the remaining end, and almost on a level with the gallery was an enclosed platform about eight feet long, from the middle of which projected a box pulpit, just wide enough for a single person. The pews were high backed and uncomfortable. When it became evident that in spite of [the] stout building, the old chapel would soon be unfit for religious service without repairs, the pastor summoned the trustees together, and an immediate renovation was decided upon. Pulpit and gallery were taken out, the ceiling was lowered, and the interior completely remodeled.

A tin roof was put on, new fences erected, and carriage sheds will be up at an early day. On Sunday, November 11, despite the inclement weather, a large congregation filled the house, and all were delighted at the transformation. "J. W. Harkins and F. M. Brady, former pastors, preached in the morning and evening, and J. T. Satchell, of Lancaster, in the afternoon. The total cost of the improvements was about $750. of which $450. has been previously provided for. During the day $320. was secured, besides a liberal quarterly collection. In the evening extra services was begun and one penitent was at the altar. A. J. Amthor is the pastor. (transcribed from microfilm records at Drew U. Library, March 5, 1985.)

[31] See History '43. p. 77f.

[32] Thanks to Henry B. Harbage (Boehm's descendent) of Philadelphia.

[33] See Appendix No. 3, reference church records.

[34] These copies have been deposited at the First UMC, Lancaster, archives room.

[35] Elizabeth E. Smith and her bachelor brother, the Hon. A. Herr Smith, both active members of First UMC, Lancaster are recorded benefactors of later 19th century Methodism around Lancaster. The Lancaster County Historical Society library biographical file tells of their relationships especially state representative A. H. Smith. E.G."in 1990 she have her house at 125 N. Duke St., Lancaster, for the Library...their father, Jacob Smith, was a prominent

millwright at Burnt Mill, Bumgardners Mill, Pequea Creek...Jacob lies buried in the Marticville UMC graveyard...they gave liberally to their home church as well as other churches..."

[36] My 1943 history observes that this was Asbury's last visit to Strasburg, and that "John Funk was the local artist there, and evidently he did a good job because Henry Boehm spoke of this picture and said it was a very likeness of the Bishop. I inquired about this picture the other day when in Strasburg. A member of the Stacy-Atmore family there reports that it has been given to some central Methodist institution in Washington, D.C. Apparently it is preserved properly somewhere."

[37] See History '43. p. 103ff.